Praise for *The Gifts* ~, ~~~~~

"Danny has written a masterpiece on the art and science of acceptance, revealing the paradoxical relationship between true acceptance and transformation—the key to serenity, vitality, clarity, love, joy, and wisdom. This is truly a gift to anyone who takes the time to read the precious words within this little book."

> —Joseph Bailey, psychologist and best-selling author of *The Serenity Principle, Slowing Down to the Speed of Life*, and other books

"I have been in long-term recovery in both Al-Anon and AA, and being willing to accept those people and situations over which I have no control is necessary to my peace of mind. Miller's book is absolutely key to understanding acceptance and how to flourish within the confines of relationships that snag our ego. I highly recommend this book to those who struggle to simply 'let people be.'"

> —Karen Casey, PhD, best-selling author of *Let Go Now, Change Your Mind and Your Life Will Follow*, and other books

"Daniel Miller shows us how acceptance is the first step toward peace. If you dwell on what you want to change about others and feel weighed down by anger, fear, and resentment, *The Gifts of Acceptance* can help set you free."

> —Lori Deschene, author of *Tiny Buddha's Gratitude Journal, Tiny Buddha's Worry Journal*, and other books

"If you think you know what acceptance means, think again. In his latest book, Danny Miller breaks down the myths and gifts of this approach to life and provides practical self-inquiries and 'acceptance intentions,' as well as real-life examples to help you handle every type of difficult relationship and circumstance with greater peace and serenity. You will keep reaching for *The Gifts of Acceptance* as one of the 12-step staples in your library."

> —Nijole Sparkis, spiritual coach and host of the *Heal the Shadow in Your Relationships* series

Praise for *Losing Control, Finding Serenity*

"Daniel A. Miller has done an amazing job in delving deeply into the crevices of how most of us need to be in control. He has created a way of guiding and educating the reader, in a very understandable and logical way, to help everyone 'Let Go.' A must read for everyone!"

—*In Light Times*

"Down-to-earth and honest, the book is full of psychological and spiritual insight. It is also full of real world solutions for reconnecting with the natural flow of life and with our personal truth."

—*New Age Retailer*

"Reading Miller's words really helped me to understand the many ways control plays a part in my life—and he offered some great advice on how to let go of the need for control."

—*Dani DiPirro, Positively Present*

"*Losing Control, Finding Serenity* pinpoints the dangers of excessive control. It shows those of us who feel the pressure to control how to break free and reap unexpected gifts. Drawing on psychological insights, spiritual wisdom, and the real-life stories of acknowledged control freaks, the author guides us through an honest inventory of our control patterns, leading us to discover this compulsion is provoked by deep-seated fear, anxiety, and insecurity, then aggravated by anger and resentments. In a chaotic, unpredictable world that's frequently beyond our control, *Losing Control, Finding Serenity* offers welcome encouragement and validation for going with the flow of life as it is: an ongoing, ever changing mystery."

—*The Monthly Aspectarian*

THE GIFTS OF ACCEPTANCE

ALSO BY DANIEL A. MILLER

Losing Control, Finding Serenity:
How the Need to Control Hurts Us
and How to Let It Go

How to Invest in Real Estate Syndicates

THE GIFTS OF ACCEPTANCE

*Embracing People and Things
as They Are*

Daniel A. Miller

Ebb and Flow Press
Sherman Oaks, California

Ebb and Flow Press
13547 Ventura Blvd., PMB 93
Sherman Oaks, California 91423

Cataloging-in-Publication data

Names: Miller, Daniel Aaron, 1943-, author.
Title: The gifts of acceptance : embracing people and things as
   they are / Daniel A. Miller.
Description: Includes bibliographical references and index. |
   Sherman Oaks, CA: Ebb and Flow Press, 2018.
Identifiers: ISBN 978-0-9828930-5-0 | LCCN 2017915870
Subjects: LCSH Self-acceptance. | Happiness. | Self-actualization
   (Psychology) | Self-help techniques. | Interpersonal
   relationships. | Mental health. | Self-management (Psychology)
   | Conduct of life. | BISAC SELF-HELP / Personal Growth
   / Happiness | BODY, MIND & SPIRIT / Inspiration and
   Personal Growth
Classification: LCC BF575.H27 .M51 2018| DDC 158--dc23

Text and cover design by Bookwrights
Printed in the United States of America

First Edition
23 22 21 20 19 18   10 9 8 7 6 5 4 3 2 1

The Space Between

Vacuum of the unknown,
Uneven compass
From Entrance to Exit, and
Thought to action.

Abode to worry and anxiety,
Suffering abyss when our
Wants aren't of this Moment,
And our fears can't find their courage.

A translucent Shrine,
Sensed vaguely as
The Space Between
And seen only as
"   "
Yet in its Halls
Expectations cease,
Interests align,
Denial discovers Awareness,
Resistance shrinks to Acceptance, and
Our quest for Serenity eases as
Real Truth Reveals.

Daniel A. Miller

CONTENTS

Part IV. Accepting Ourselves

For after all, the best thing one can do
When it is raining, is to let it rain.

—*Henry Wadsworth Longfellow,*
"The Birds of Killingworth," 1863

MY PATH FROM CONTROL TO ACCEPTANCE

FOR MOST OF MY adult life, I was a controller extraordinaire. I firmly believed that the best way to satisfy my needs and achieve what I wanted in life was by controlling everything and everyone. I constantly directed, pressed, and persisted, trying to change others. In my "infinite wisdom," I believed that I knew what was best for them, especially those closest to me. I even believed I was acting benevolently in doing so. At home, Father truly knew best; at work, I was a taskmaster who hovered over everyone to make sure they did things my way.

Back then, the idea of accepting people and things as they were was the furthest thing from my mind. Controllers simply don't accept things as they are.

By most standards, you could say I was successful. I graduated with high honors from a top law school, later developed and taught college-level real estate courses, and wrote a best-selling book on real estate investing. I also owned a real estate investment company with well-known celebrities and the wealthy as clients.

Yet deep inside—in my core—I didn't feel successful or content. How could I? I was constantly enmeshed in worries, anxieties, and deep fears. Such is the fate of most controllers.

The catalyst for my discovering the profound benefits of acceptance was my suffering through a rapid-fire series of traumatic events thirty-five years ago that shook me to my core. It started with a major mudslide at our house following eight days of unusually bad weather in Los Angeles. I woke up to see our newly built fifty-foot deck dangling halfway down the hill, precariously close to a neighbor's house. Weeks later, a mentally disturbed neighbor set a fire in our garage, directly below my eight-year-old son Brandon's bedroom. The fire singed my car and came within an inch of the gas cap before I doused it, barely averting a total disaster.

The incident so unnerved my first wife that she began sleeping in our son's room. We installed a burglar and fire alarm system and, for added measure, bought a police-trained guard dog. We couldn't move from our house because we couldn't sell it. There was still mudslide damage to be repaired and we didn't have the funds to repair it.

Soon afterward, I was betrayed by a business partner intent on squeezing me out of my most profitable real estate investment. He controlled the purse strings and began withholding the money due me from the investment. He also made disparaging remarks about me and my wife to our banker. The problem was, we shared the same banker—my partner introduced us—and my partner happened to be one of the bank's wealthiest clients.

The bank called my loans—well in excess of a million dollars today—and I didn't have the means to repay them. The sudden deterioration of my financial condition forced me to withdraw from pending real estate deals, wiping out more than two years of income. Consumed with unbridled anger and resentment, I foolishly launched a costly five-year legal battle that brought me to the brink of bankruptcy. I was obsessed with revenge and with the foolhardy task of trying to make an honest man out of a dishonest one. I used every dollar and controlling means available to me in my efforts. Accepting this person for who he was and acting in my best interests under the circumstances was not even a consideration.

At this low point, rather than face up and accept how my obsessive crusade had severely damaged my marriage and relationship with my son, I tried to control and fight back even more. During the next three months, one of my most successful real estate investments was completely destroyed by fire, and another suffered three robberies, one of which culminated in the shoot-out death of the robber and ensuing front-page headlines. This was followed by a mass exodus of tenants and foreclosure proceedings by the lender.

I badly needed to get away and gain some perspective, so I took Brandon on a week's vacation to Club Med in Mexico. When we returned, I went into the hospital for what I was told would be a simple twenty-minute outpatient procedure to remove a skin cancer on my right nostril. It was something I had put off while dealing with all my travails—and I ended up on the table for over three hours, followed by three major surgeries over a six-week period to eradicate the cancerous tissue, which had spread through my face like the roots of a tree. I lost half my nose and it took several more surgeries to reconstruct it. As luck would have it, my insurance coverage was dropped after the first round of surgeries.

It was only then that I was finally able to accept the folly of my control-driven life. It was time to give up. I was totally depleted. I had neither the strength nor desire to go on fighting whatever demons were going to attack me next. With that acceptance, I was able to "surrender" what I was always most secure with in my life: control. It no longer worked for me—if it ever did!

With that surrender, my control-colored blinders began to fall away. New opportunities emerged, and I was able to glimpse a more serene way of life, one that eventually led to great financial success, artistic achievements, and stronger bonds with my family. It also led to my writing an award-winning book on personal growth (*Losing Control, Finding Serenity*), in which I shared practical tools and strategies I had learned for letting go of control.

MOVING TOWARD ACCEPTANCE

As I tried to let go of control in more areas of my life, it became apparent to me that the "decontrol" tool that worked best for me was accepting "what is" about people, places, and things. I found that the more I accept my loved ones, children, friends—even my adversaries—and my life circumstances as they are, the less need I have to control. It is no longer necessary.

As time went on, I made an effort to incorporate greater acceptance into my life. I began to ponder such things as

- What if I accepted the helter-skelter way in which my youngest daughter did her homework and studied for important exams?
- What if I accepted my wife's own ways of doing things?
- What if I accepted certain friends' poor social manners?
- What if I accepted the unorthodox work practices of my business partners?
- What if I accepted the unsportsmanlike antics of certain tennis opponents?
- What if I accepted the physical limitations of getting older?
- What if I accepted that my way may not be the best or right way for others?
- What if I accepted my failures?

And indeed, most importantly,

- What if I accepted myself as I am—flaws and all?

Succeeding at these things, not surprisingly, was far more difficult than simply pondering them. It helped considerably, however, to understand that acceptance didn't mean that I had to like or condone what I accepted; only that I needed to accept its underlying "reality." (More about this important distinction later.)

As practicing acceptance expanded to more and more areas of my life, I couldn't help but notice that traversing life's ups and downs became much easier for me—at times, even smooth—and that the benefits of acceptance went well beyond reducing my need to control. Self-imposed burdens and obligations were lifted from my shoulders, resulting in reduced stress, anxiety, and worry. There was greater trust, openness, and intimacy with my loved ones and friends. I enjoyed real communication and connection with my three children—indeed, I was able to truly appreciate their unique talents as well as learn from them. It also strengthened bonds with my coworkers and business partners. It even enabled me to avoid disputes and dodge the "arrows" of my perceived foes and adversaries.

Very significantly, I found that practicing acceptance was an unexpectedly strong catalyst for revealing new choices and opportunities, particularly when I felt stuck or discouraged.

An even greater awareness of these gifts came from speaking and participating in life transformation forums and personal recovery workshops, where I saw firsthand the often life-changing rewards of acceptance. Indeed, acceptance is the very essence of the Serenity Prayer and the first step of the 12-step programs widely attended throughout the world. I also read about recent studies that strongly supported the life and health benefits of acceptance.

PEOPLE YEARN TO PRACTICE ACCEPTANCE

During this time, I began sharing on my blog some of the things I was learning about the acceptance dynamic and how to effectively practice it.[1] Reader response was strong and immediate. My acceptance posts and articles became the most highly read and commented upon ones on the blog—by far. One post titled "Five Reasons for Accepting People as They Are" has frequently been at the top of the first page of Google search results on the subject of acceptance for over five years.

It became clear to me that the acceptance paradigm resonated strongly with people from all walks of life and that people genuinely want to be able to accept their children, mates, parents, siblings, and friends, as well as their life circumstances, but often struggle mightily to do so.

Take Leslie, a regular visitor to my blog, for example. From a young age, she longed for contact from her dad after he moved and remarried following his divorce from her mother. Well into her adult years, she waited anxiously for a phone call on her birthday and an "I love you." When her father came to town, she hoped that he would call and want to see her. When these things didn't happen, she was always shattered. She wondered,

"What did I do wrong? Why does he not want to be with me? How could he love his other family more?

"Until one day, I saw my dad for who he was, and *accepted* his shortcomings. . . . I began not to 'expect.' I was then able to let go of all the anger, and all the things he was *not doing* somehow started to happen. Birthday cards, lunch dates when he was in town, and frequent phone calls."

Thus, by finally accepting her father for how he was, Leslie was blessed with the caring connection for which she yearned.

ACCEPTANCE STORIES

Leslie's story is not unique. In the pages that follow, you will read other inspirational stories like hers, ones that reveal how people have been graced by the gifts of acceptance in myriad ways and circumstances, some through struggle and adversity, others through happenstance, and some from personal epiphanies. Many only came to acceptance after enduring the pains and discomforts of denial and resentment, and almost all through awareness, self-honesty, and the willingness and courage to change ways that no longer worked for them.

You will read, for example:

- How a young woman's acceptance of her debilitating bipolar condition blessed her with greater brightness in her good days and less pain during her bad ones.

- How a former drug addict's acceptance that his parents didn't intentionally try to harm him psychologically allowed him to stop blaming them for his shortcomings and take personal responsibility for improving his life.

- How a controlling father's acceptance that he didn't always know what was best for his children brought him the joy of seeing his children's "harebrained schemes" turn into wise choices.

- How a man's accepting that his ambivalent girlfriend could not make the commitment he wanted enabled him to confront and work through his long-standing issues of loneliness and abandonment.

- How a young man's acceptance of his pronounced stuttering—which plagued him since he was three years old—led to professional accomplishments and a loving wife and children.

- How a bright college student, in accepting unforeseen scholastic failures, discovered previously unknown resiliency and feelings of self-worth.

- How an adult daughter's acceptance that her mother couldn't give her the support that, as a child, she so badly needed resulted in profound bonding and intimacy during her mother's final days—indeed, more than she could ever have imagined.

- How a man's living in daily acceptance of the life-altering injuries from a near-fatal motorcycle accident enabled him to look forward to a life filled with new hopes and aspirations.

- How a graphic artist's acceptance of an unfriendly loner in the same department of a large media company resulted in a lasting friendship in which they shared a common passion for metal sculpture work.

You will also read about how people who were overwhelmed by their loved ones' drug and alcohol addictions finally accepted that they were powerless over changing them. They were not only relieved of guilt and great burdens but also were able to improve their own lives by taking better care of themselves.

THE CHALLENGES OF PRACTICING ACCEPTANCE

Recognizing the benefits of acceptance is not difficult. Practicing it can feel like a major challenge. For example, unexpected job and financial setbacks, the limitations and frailties that come with getting older, the breakup of a marriage or close friendship, and the character flaws and addictions of our children and siblings are all difficult to accept. It's also often a constant struggle merely to accept the annoying traits of our mates or parents.

Acceptance of oneself can be the greatest challenge of all. Denial, self-justification, and lack of humility and self-honesty prevent us from acknowledging our shortcomings. Shame, insecurity, and low self-esteem deprive us from recognizing our personal qualities. Hence, we often have little understanding of who our true "self" is. The final two chapters of this book shed light on the truths and paradoxes of self-acceptance and offer ways of accepting ourselves more fully.

In most instances, we must overcome formidable obstacles, such as fears, bitterness, and anxieties about discordant relationships and trying circumstances. So, too, we must restrain our strong ego and constant need to be right. Another barrier is our propensity to deny—

whether because of our lack of awareness or wishful thinking—the unpleasant "what is," rather than facing the difficult "truth," and lest we overlook it, the impediment of our unrealistically high expectations.

It thus comes as no surprise that many people—maybe even you—feel or believe that practicing acceptance is too difficult, maybe even impossible, or simply not worth all the effort it takes. Others feel they would have to give up too much of themselves, particularly their values, goals, and high standards. We will see later, however, that this is not the case and that acceptance and our core values are more complementary than exclusionary. Still, for many, it is much easier to control, resist, and justify almost anything except accept their powerlessness over changing others and most things.

TOOLS AND STRATEGIES FOR PRACTICING ACCEPTANCE

One of my reasons for writing this book is to assist you in overcoming these challenges and obstacles so that you, too, can enjoy the certain rewards that will follow. I lay out practical tools and strategies learned through personal experiences—both successes and setbacks—with my loved ones, children, friends, coworkers, and foes, as well as those inspired by the stories, insights, and wisdom others have shared at various meetings and workshops and in articles and posts on websites. Speaking, studying, and writing on this subject and the control dynamic have also taught me quite a bit, and I include these lessons as well. It has helped me to mentor people with control and acceptance issues. Recent research on the subject provides constructive guidance as well.

My recommendations are made with a deep sense of humility, for I know how difficult it can be to apply them in the midst of crisis and major setbacks. To this day, I continually struggle—and fail—with acceptance issues. However, I take solace that with willingness and trust, I continue to learn and improve. Indeed, learning to live in acceptance is a lifelong endeavor, one in which we can be grateful for the gifts we receive with even partial successes.

You will see, too, that as you continue practicing acceptance, your mind-set will change from one of resistance, refusal, and denial to awareness, trust, and acceptance. As you begin to receive the gifts of acceptance in more settings and situations, your life will be transformed in often wondrous and unforeseen ways, making it possible for you to establish more soulful connections with others, with life in general—and with yourself.

ACCEPTANCE IS A CHOICE

Fundamentally, acceptance is a *choice* we make. You can choose to accept people and circumstances as they are, or not. If you choose acceptance, that very act births opportunities that can transform—often dramatically—your life, the lives of others, and, I believe, the world. In doing so, you will come to understand—and *know*—that the blessings of acceptance are bountiful! In the truest sense, acceptance is the path to peace and serenity.

My hope is that this book will make it easier for you to make this choice.

PART I

EMBRACING LIFE
AS IT IS

CHAPTER ONE

THE SERENITY OF LIVING IN ACCEPTANCE

Serenity is not freedom from the storm,
but peace amid the storm.

—Unknown Author

GREG WAS ONLY FORTY-SEVEN when his life changed in a split second in the early morning of April 29, 2013. As he did every weekday morning, Greg hopped on his motorcycle to ride from Reseda, in Los Angeles's San Fernando Valley, to Long Beach, California, where he worked as a geology compliance consultant to oil companies. This particular morning, however, he took a different side street to the nearby lighted intersection leading to the freeway. A car traveling in the opposite direction made a sudden left turn into his lane, crashing into him—and that was the last thing Greg remembers.

He awakened from a coma two weeks later. It wasn't until a month had passed that Greg began to realize what had happened to him—initially a broken pelvis and punched-out hip socket; compound fractures to his right tibia, fibula, ankle, and wrist; a severe concussion; and blood clots. After spending three months in a rehab facility followed by four months in a wheelchair and additional physical therapy, Greg was able to walk a few feet at a time with the aid of a walker.

I met with Greg at his home three years after the accident. He was able to walk with a crutch but still couldn't move his right leg because of severe nerve damage that rendered his quadriceps useless. He was scheduled for surgery in three weeks to repair three extensive hernias caused by improper stitching after the accident. Greg had recently shared at a men's discussion group that we both attended that the only way he was able to get by was by "living in acceptance each and every day."

No longer able to work as a geologist, Greg told me his "new job" was to get better—one day at a time. He said he prayed and meditated on acceptance the first thing every morning. "I meditate on where I was, where I am, and where I'm going," he said. When I asked him if he could expand on that further, he replied:

"I have a lot of limitations. But I don't think about what I can't do. I need to think about how I'm *not* limited. Just last week I went fishing for the first time in three years, and it was an absolute blast—and I caught a ton of fish! Acceptance builds on itself, like a snowball. But if I don't remain positive in that way, I start feeling sorry for myself, and that only sets me back. If I don't practice acceptance, I get mired down in the problems and can't find the solutions. The way I look at it, I have to accept where I'm at to get to where I want to go."

As Greg talked, I commented that he seemed so open and positive about the future, even grateful. He replied,

"Yes. By accepting where I'm at, I get to practice gratitude for what I can do. And I am looking forward to where I get to go next. I get to start again. A new career. A new life."

Greg's story exemplifies the serenity that comes by living in acceptance, even under the most difficult of circumstances. Although we may not have his remarkable positivity and courage, greater serenity is still possible, even if we are able to live in acceptance for only part of the time. A strong commitment and willingness to try will be rewarded.

In our important relationships, accepting others as they are—even those we dislike or have made our life harder—brings greater serenity. Martin's life got better, for example, after he stopped blaming his parents for his personal shortcomings.

Martin Accepts His Parents as They Are

Well into his adulthood, Martin blamed his parents for his insecurities, low self-esteem, and people-pleasing tendencies. His father was an alcoholic who was rarely around and his mother constantly demeaned him. Whatever Martin did was never "good enough" for her. As a result, growing up, he never felt good about himself. In fact, as Martin puts it, he wasn't sure who "himself" really was. Consequently, by his early twenties, he was an alcoholic and street druggie, in and out of treatment centers and sober living homes.

In his mid-thirties, Martin found sobriety in Alcoholics Anonymous and a few years later joined

Al-Anon, another 12-step program for those whose family or friends have drinking problems. There he gained a greater awareness of "self" and what made him tick. One of the things Martin learned was that blaming his parents for his struggles was absolutely of no benefit to him now. Pure and simple, it neither helped nor made him feel better. To the contrary, he says it deterred him from working on his personal shortcomings.

Martin speaks about how his life improved by accepting his parents for who they were:

"I certainly didn't like what my parents did when I was young. It messed me up a lot. But I know for sure that they didn't go to bed at night thinking, 'Now what can we do tomorrow to make Martin's life miserable?' And I also know for sure that they didn't have any mean or evil intent. That's just the way they were; they didn't know any better. I am in acceptance of that now. My primary focus now is working on *myself.* It's solely up to me to make my life better. I'm finally getting to know who 'Martin' is and finding a lot that I like."

It's never too late to benefit from accepting things as they are. Janice learned this in encountering unplanned changes later in life.

AN OVERBURDENED GRANDPARENT IS REWARDED

Janice loves her two grandchildren dearly, but her role in their lives is far different from what she imagined it would be. Her vision of grandparenting included the carefree joy of seeing them primarily at family gatherings and taking them on special outings. This did not come to pass. Janice and her husband, Mark, both in their late sixties, have been raising their two grandchildren, due to their daughter's severe drug and alcohol addictions.

Janice's retirement hasn't been anything like she had planned either. The family finances are stretched thin and she's almost always tired. She has little privacy of her own, can't take vacations alone with Mark, and hardly ever enjoys an evening out with friends.

Yet, what is so noticeable about Janice is that she doesn't complain or display any bitterness over her situation. She always seems so serene. Indeed, when she speaks, it's in a soft-spoken, matter-of-fact manner. In explaining how she manages so well, Janice says in her typically humble manner:

"I've learned to accept what's happened. When I didn't at first, I had no serenity at all. Only remorse and anger and constant fights with my husband and my daughter when I saw her. So, for me, there really was no choice but to accept that we would be the ones responsible for raising our two grandchildren and all that entails. That wasn't an easy decision, to be sure, but it was the reality, and I have much less stress and anxiety than I did when I was trying to fight it. And sure, it's not what I had expected or wanted, but you know, I have to say that we've been blessed with so many unexpected things. I now get to help my grandchildren with their homework, share with them my life experiences and learnings, and be involved in their youthful adventures—and misadventures! Yes, life's a lot different at this stage in my life than I thought it would be, but it's still good!"

THE SERENITY OF LIVING IN ACCEPTANCE

These stories and others that you will read later demonstrate the integral relationship between accepting life and people as they are and enjoying a life with greater serenity. It leads to a life marked by realistic expectations, greater humility, and new choices, discoveries, and possibilities, as well as reduced worry, stress, and frustration—a life where hope replaces despair.

Moreover, these gifts are bestowed not only on us. When we accept others as they are, we are offering them one of the most important gifts that we can: unconditional love and friendship. Take a moment and think about how good it feels when a loved one or a friend accepts you just as you are—shortcomings, quirks, and all. Really, really good, right? It makes it easier to just be yourself, comfortable in your "own skin," so to speak. It also releases you from the need to be a people pleaser in order to be accepted by others.

Knowing that we have helped others or made them feel better is also deeply gratifying. In that sense, the gifts of acceptance are reciprocal. It's truly a win-win situation. Consequently, as you make an effort to accept more people and things in your life using the tools in this book, try to keep in mind that what you are doing is likely helping them in their personal life struggles. This makes practicing acceptance even more meaningful.

Let's next take a look at some of the specific gifts that are a natural consequence of living in acceptance.

CHAPTER TWO

THE GIFTS OF ACCEPTANCE

Not everything that is faced can be changed; but
nothing can be changed until it is faced.
— *James Baldwin, American Novelist*[1]

THERE IS A GOOD reason why dogs are considered
man's best friends. They offer us unconditional *acceptance!* Even when we're mad at them, they accept us—
usually with wagging tails!

Now with people, that's quite a different story. We
are not nearly as accepting of others, particularly when
they irritate us by their annoying habits and traits.

Do you think our canine friends know something
we don't?

Perhaps, if we considered some of the significant
benefits of accepting others and things as they are, we
might be more willing to try.

STRONGER BONDS AND CONNECTION

When I first met Anna, she was constantly being undermined by her mother, Emma, an only child who immigrated to the United States from the "old country" after World War II. Emma was ill-equipped to raise her five children in a culturally diverse country, and she made no bones about not enjoying being a mom. Anna was a dutiful daughter who dearly wanted a nurturing mother and thus continually looked to Emma for support and encouragement, but it rarely came. Instead, Anna received criticism and demeaning remarks from her mother. Yet well into her adult life, Anna persisted in seeking what her mother was unable to give her. She always received the same results.

Then one day, Anna had an epiphany that dramatically changed the relationship between the two women. Anna saw a movie in which the heroine was viciously attacked, and the first person she called for help was her mother. This made an impression on Anna. She realized that her own mother would have been the *last* person she would call under similar circumstances. From that turning point, Anna began to accept her mother for who she was—and just as important, for who she wasn't! Because she did this, Anna also stopped trying to get from her mother that which could not be given. Interestingly, Anna and her mother's relationship improved dramatically. The pressure was off Emma to be someone she wasn't. Over time, the two became friends and equals, and Emma began to open up more to her daughter. She even shared her feelings about growing older. When Emma later became gravely ill, Anna was there to share her mother's final intimate moments, a time in which they discussed the selection of songs and prayers, even the clothes and personal jewelry to be worn, at Emma's funeral.

In these hectic, impersonal times, the need for intimate, close bonds and connection with friends, family and loved ones is more important than ever for our overall well-being. When people know that you truly accept them, they don't feel pressured or judged or "less than." Trust develops and they feel safer in opening up to you, as Emma did with Anna.

Anna's story also illustrates the strong link between control, acceptance, and intimacy. When we try to change or control others, there is almost always a loss of intimacy and connection. The fact that we feel our controlling intentions may be "good" for them doesn't change that. We are still being intrusive. Conversely, when we are accepting of others, there is no need to try to change them.

The dynamic between control and acceptance is much like trying to connect two magnets. If each magnet has one side infused with control and the opposite with acceptance, placing the two acceptance sides together forges a very strong bond. However, when you place the two control sides together, it causes a forceful separation. In much the same manner, acceptance brings people closer together, whereas control pushes them apart.

GREATER FREEDOM

When Chris had a chronic illness, all his efforts were dedicated toward getting well. He says he spent "tons" of energy researching possible causes of his symptoms. Chris tried special diets and took supplements, herbs and drugs. He saw numerous doctors and alternative practitioners of every possible persuasion and read every health book he could get his hands on.

Despite all these efforts, he didn't fully recover his health. He finally accepted that his illness was not "solvable" and that it would always be with him in some form. His acceptance, however, removed what he calls the "unnecessary layer of suffering" that came from continuously struggling against what was his objective reality. Moreover, it brought about a new sense of freedom for him.

As Chris simply explains:

"When we accept what is, we are free. Free to act in accordance with reality. Free to be at peace with the circumstances of our lives, no matter how undesirable or difficult they are."[2]

Tiny Buddha contributor Iva Ursano found freedom when she finally forgave her father for the severe beatings she received from the time she was ten years old until she fled home as an eighteen-year-old. To be sure, it didn't come easy or without a struggle intertwined with a lot of bitterness. Iva relates:

"I spent most of my adult years trying to forgive him, like him, maybe even love him a little. The forgiving finally came. Liking and loving, not so much. It was clear in my thirties, forties, and into my fifties that I simply did not like my father. Not one bit. Because of that I lived daily with this monkey on my back. This thorn in my side. Guilt in my soul."

Yet remembering that he did provide her shelter, food, clothes, money when she was broke, and nice family vacations, she bravely forgave him and made an effort to show him some love. She visited him when he was in a nursing home, hugged him, and even said "I love you Daddy," all the while thinking maybe it was a lie.

In explaining how she was able to forgive and accept her father for who he was and the freedom that came with that, Iva shares:

"When Dad died at eighty-eight, I cried tears of relief and closure. But it wasn't his death that set me free—it was the choice to forgive and treat him with more kindness than he offered me. I knew then the pain hadn't scarred me for life. I had taken that pain and turned it into strength and wisdom. I forgave him because I could finally see he raised me the only way he knew how. That's all he knew—it was how he was raised. . . .

"Did it make it okay? No. Understanding doesn't mean we condone it when someone hurts us. It means we understand. And understanding and compassion are the keys to forgiveness."[3]

As these stories illustrate, once we have accepted the things that we cannot change or control, we are no longer *bound* by them. Simply put, *when you accept "what is," you are free to discover "what might be."*

NEW CHOICES AND OPPORTUNITIES

Karl got very frustrated when he couldn't physically do what he wanted because of a worsening glaucoma condition. Photography had always been his first love, but at seventy-nine and with deteriorating vision, he no longer could pursue his passion. "My limitations were very, very severe and it took a while before I realized that I could no longer do what was in my mind," Karl confessed. Yet when he finally accepted he could no longer be an active photographer, an unexpected new path revealed itself—one that he admits would not have arisen otherwise.[4]

Karl became a photography teacher. Even though he could no longer perform the skills he had before his glaucoma, he retained the knowledge and ability to teach others how to take good photos, and this became his gratifying new passion. Karl's story illustrates one of the most significant blessings of practicing acceptance: it creates new choices and opportunities.

That's because acceptance expands your vision.

When you don't accept things as they are, it is akin to keeping a lid on choices and opportunities that can improve your life, often dramatically. Acceptance removes your blinders and you can recognize choices and opportunities that were invisible to you before. Your focus is changed from what you can't change or control in another or about a situation to what you can do to make things better. In a very real sense, it allows you to see the beauty all around you. The following story shared with me by my friend Michael illustrates this well:

"Late one night I was taking out a load of trash. I was really tired when I got home after working late. I had to clean up after my daughter and baby grandchild who were living with us, and I was resentful about having no time to myself. As I was outside at the trash bin, a thought went through me, coming from nowhere: '*This is the moment I'm living in.*' I looked up at the crescent moon, the lights of the house, and our cat, Chanel, moving in the darkness. It was all quite beautiful and calming. That was a kind of prayer of acceptance. I now use it often."

LESS STRESS, FRUSTRATION, AND WORRY

Jenna needed to buy some last-minute holiday gifts at her local mall and encountered nerve-racking obstacles common during that time of the year. First, she had to join a block-long line of cars creeping along toward the parking entrance. Once entering, she had to maneuver like a matador to avoid cars aggressively vying for parking spaces as if they were winning lottery tickets. Walking into the department store, Jenna then had to navigate through hordes of frenzied shoppers and clothes strewn about as if there had been a teenage slumber party the night before. After finally finding the things she was looking for, she had to wait fifteen minutes before it was her turn at the cashier counter.

After hearing her story, I remarked that she must have been totally stressed out by the experience. To my surprise, Jenna responded, "No, not really."

Knowing that my emotional equilibrium would be off kilter if I had endured the same obstacles, I asked her how she managed to remain so calm in the midst of such madness. Without missing a beat, she replied, "If I'm entering the madness, I have to accept that's all part of it."

True words, indeed. The underlying reality is that the holidays are truly maddening times for most people. Heavy traffic, rude people, too few sales clerks, family dinners with estranged siblings, and so on. Jenna was wise enough to recognize that she was powerless over changing any of that and thus wasn't overwhelmed by it all.

PEOPLE STRESSORS

Acceptance is not just a "destressor" of trying situations. It also insulates us from people stressors, such as intimidating bosses, control freaks, and other "crazy-makers." When we are able to accept such people as they are, their actions and words cause us considerably less stress and anxiety. As we will see in part II, acceptance allows us to disengage and remove ourselves from them and not take things personally—and sometimes even "forgive" their trespasses, for they likely do not know what they do!

THE STRESS/FRUSTRATION/ ACCEPTANCE DYNAMIC

Dr. Erin Olivo, an assistant clinical professor in medical psychology at Columbia University, says when we deny or ignore our distressing emotions, we create stress, and acceptance reduces stress because it helps us manage those emotions. She shares, "If you want to stop stressing, you need to be in charge of your emotions and. . . . acceptance is the quickest route there."[5]

In a similar vein, writer Stephanie Harper says our life expectations and frustrations go hand-in-hand, when our expectations are not met because of ever-changing circumstances, frustrations result. She says while she still dreams and strives to work hard for the life she wants for herself, she has learned that at times she needs to let go of those expectations and just go with what's happening in her life. Stephanie says, "It's in this space of acceptance that I can begin to put my frustrations in check and just live."[6]

There perhaps is an even more basic reason why acceptance reduces stress and frustration. When we accept things as they are, it feels as if a heavy burden is lifted from our shoulders. We no longer have to worry or obsess over them. That allows us to breathe easier and focus on the realistic choices we have under the circumstances, and with that, we no longer feel so "stuck," which lessens our stress even more.

The simple truth is that with acceptance, little really remains to stress over.

You may be thinking, yeah, that's all good and dandy, but it's much easier said than done. I can understand your skepticism. I've felt that way, too. However, it makes it easier if you are mindful that acceptance is simply surrendering that which you never had—control.

Not having control, that's a hard one, too. (Indeed, I wrote a book on that recurrent challenge!) But it's important to accept that truth as well. So what is there to lose by practicing acceptance? The short answer is *nothing*! The long answer is *a lot of stress*!

THE BEST ANTIDOTE FOR CONTROL

When we are accepting of others or things, there no longer is a need for us to try to change or control them. The very act of acceptance removes that need, and our focus is redirected to where it should rightly (and most productively) be: *ourselves.*

I thus like to say:

"*When you are controlling, you aren't accepting,*" and "*When you are accepting, you aren't controlling.*"

As such, control and acceptance are inextricably intertwined. They are different sides of the same coin. It is no coincidence that many of the stories in this book about the acceptance dynamic also include aspects of the control dynamic. It is also no coincidence that letting go of control and accepting "what is" facilitate one another, and doing both blesses us and others with even greater serenity.

These gifts of acceptance, as well as others, will be more apparent and explored in greater depth as we later look at ways of how to accept our loved ones, children, family, friends, and others, as well as our limitations and life adversities. But first, it's important to have a clear understanding of what true acceptance is—and isn't. It is both *more* and *less* than you might think.

CHAPTER THREE

WHAT ACCEPTANCE IS— AND ISN'T!

> Acceptance doesn't mean resignation;
> it means understanding that something
> is what it is and that there's got to be
> a way through it.
>
> —*Michael J. Fox, American actor* [1]

IF YOU ARE LIKE others I have spoken to about accepting annoying people in their lives, your thoughts on the subject might be similar to theirs:

Why should I accept . . .

My sister's condescending behavior?
My mother's belittling me all the time?
My husband's telling me what's best for me?
My boss's nitpicking ways?
My opponent's unsportsmanlike conduct?

If pressed to at least try accepting such people as they are, they might respond with something like

Why should I have to put up with it?
What good will it do me?
I don't need them in my life.
I refuse to sacrifice my principles and values.
Nothing will really change.

These are all very valid concerns, and truth be told, I've felt them many times myself. However, I have learned that they stem mainly from certain misconceptions about what acceptance means. To give you more comfort about acceptance, let's look at some of its common misperceptions.

Acceptance does *not* mean

- **That you approve or condone another's behavior or the situation.** It is a mistake to equate acceptance with approval. As with Iva's finally accepting her abusive father in the previous chapter, you are not approving or condoning anybody or anything by accepting. Rather, you are simply acknowledging the "reality" of the person or situation and acting upon or deciding what's best for you aligned with that reality. Hence, you can accept someone or something even though you disapprove of what the person has done or the way something is. As such, acceptance is neither a positive or negative mind-set; it is a neutral one.

  However, to be very clear, acceptance does not mean that you should accept abuse, violence, or other aberrant or intolerable behavior. Nor does it mean that you cannot or should not remove yourself from, or even sever ties with, someone if

you determine that is in your best interest to do
so. As we will see later, what is important is the
manner in which you do so.

- **That you must "give in" to others or things.**
Acceptance also does not require that you relinquish your needs or subordinate your best interests to those of others or situations. Once again,
if you feel unfairly burdened or imposed upon,
you can disengage or detach—and when necessary, stand your ground. The only thing that I
believe you should give in to is that every person
has her own life path and that it is beyond your
power (and, I believe, right) to meaningfully alter
it. If your respective paths are not in sync, you
are free to acknowledge that and move on.

- **That you cannot have reasonable expectations or
set boundaries.** Acceptance does not mean that
you cannot have reasonable expectations about
how you are treated by others, nor does it pre-
clude you from setting boundaries in your interactions or engagements with people. Indeed, you
should. It's more a matter of "live and let live."

- **That you cannot be angry or resentful.** It's normal and understandable—only "human" if you
will—to be upset or resentful when someone
mistreats you or when you have to endure trying circumstances. It is important, however, to
address these strong feelings in a timely manner
and not allow them to linger too long. When they
do, you will dwell in negativity and in the past
and not be able to see the meaningful choices and

courses of action available to you. Like Martin in the first chapter, true acceptance is possible only after you stop playing the blame game and rid yourself of deeply rooted anger and resentment. We will look at some ways to do that later.

- **That you must surrender to your "lot" in life.** Acceptance does not mean that you must be so resigned to your situation that you cannot explore ways of improving your stead. We will see that acceptance often involves taking action—just in a realistic, constructive manner.

And very importantly, acceptance does *not* mean

- **That you have no viable choices.** To the contrary, like Chris in dealing with his chronic illness in the previous chapter and Janice in coping with being a grandmother/parent in the first chapter, it is only by accepting situations or circumstances as they are that you are able to recognize the choices and options that will serve you best. Why? Because with acceptance, the focus changes from others and circumstances to *you*—and what you can do to better your life.

With a better understanding of what acceptance is *not,* we can now look at what true acceptance *is.* True acceptance means accepting people and things as they are *without* judgment or harboring negative feelings such as fear, anger, resentment, and the like. As such, it is the detached, even-keeled acknowledgment of the *underlying reality*—the "how is" and "what is"—of the person or situation. Simply put, it is embracing life as it is. Self-improvement blogger Donna Torbico aptly describes this kind of acceptance as "acknowledging the TRUTH about things, without any make-up."[2]

To be clear, though, true acceptance does *not* mean that an undesirable condition or circumstance or unpleasant person will change or go away; it *does* mean, however, that our self-defeating attitudes and negative feelings will lessen or even leave, thereby allowing space for more light and joy to come into our lives.

While the meaning of true acceptance may seem clear and simple enough, practicing it in different areas of our lives often is not. Indeed, in many instances, acceptance will seem unfathomable to you. In fact, you might ask the question below.

Why Should I Accept the "Unacceptable"?

If something is unacceptable to you, you shouldn't accept it. Acceptance is a personal choice each one of us needs to make. However, what is unacceptable for one person might not be for another. Moreover, the passage of time and our own shifting viewpoint can change what was initially unacceptable to us. The determination is usually based on one's beliefs, values, and experiences and also on one's fears, anxieties, resentments, perceptions—and misperceptions.

Whatever your predisposition, however, I would offer that before you determine something or somebody to be totally unacceptable, you should first consider what doing that will accomplish (maybe nothing) and what adverse consequences could result—for you and others. A personal case in point: When a close friend was ten years old, his father totally severed ties with his brother-in-law because he felt betrayed by this person in a joint business enterprise. As a result, the two families permanently "separated," and my friend was no longer able to see his closest cousins. He said, "This was a significant loss and has impacted our relationships to this day."

At times acceptance seems near impossible in dealing with tragic events and circumstances. Tom Smith, whose adult daughter suffered from a personality disorder and took her life, describes the obstacles in reaching some degree of acceptance in extreme cases in his insightful book, *A Balanced Life: Nine Strategies for Coping with the Mental Health Problems of a Loved One:*

"Acceptance can be difficult because it forces us to deal with reality—a slippery concept. What is real and what is illusion? Whose reality are we talking about? What is the concrete, definitive truth of our life, and what is fantasy, naïve expectation, or unrealistic wish? These questions are not just for philosophers, poets, and pundits. In the special circumstances we live in, we all face these questions every day. We seldom ask them directly, but we often think, feel, and act as if we know the answers, when, in fact, we don't. . . .

"When we do assess our real abilities and limitations honestly and critically, we often see that we have less control than we thought. A sudden illness, an unexpected death, the unwanted end of a relationship, a child growing up and resisting our guidance, a person who makes choices we don't approve of, a loved one in trouble who refuses our help, a friend who disappoints us . . . all these real-life experiences expose our own limits and vulnerability. And we don't like it."[3]

RADICAL ACCEPTANCE

To help people process such horrific adversities, some psychotherapists recommend that their clients practice "radical acceptance" as a means of living a life with meaning and satisfaction even with a painful event. Clients are encouraged to consciously decide to accept reality rather than push against it. Dr. Marsha Linehan, who is at the forefront of practicing radical acceptance, describes it as letting go of the illusion of control and having the willingness to notice and accept things as they are right now, without judgment. She says the process involves accepting the reality for what it is, accepting that the event or circumstance causing you pain has a cause, and finally accepting life can still be worthwhile even with painful events in it.[4]

As such, radical acceptance includes the key elements of practicing acceptance that I write about in this book. In a sense, it can be viewed as "extraordinary" acceptance because it deals with trying to accept extraordinary events.

PRACTICING ACCEPTANCE

Be encouraged by the fact that the challenges of acceptance lessen considerably with practice. That is why I use the term "practicing acceptance." Pure and simple, embracing life as it is takes lots of practice. It needs our constant awareness and balanced perspective.

Practicing acceptance is akin to changing your muscle memory when you want to get better at your favorite sport. As an avid tennis player, I am always trying to improve my game, and my forehand has been my weakest stroke. In taking lessons from a top tournament player, I learned that my stroke fundamentals were wrong. While I understood what corrections the instructor said I needed to make to improve my forehand, my muscle memory—and my "mental" memory—were deeply ingrained from years of hitting incorrectly. It took hours of continued practice to overcome my old stroke pattern and transition into proper form. However, my forehand gradually improved and I began winning more matches and eventually some tournaments.

The same dynamic applies with acceptance. We need to change our mental muscle memory—those deeply ingrained attitudes and patterns of judging, denying, fearing, resenting, expecting, and controlling. It, too, takes lots of practice. With willingness, commitment— and courage—acceptance will become easier and more natural for you. Don't worry about lapses or setbacks. Even partial or limited success produces tremendous benefits.

FACING THE CHALLENGE

Whatever discomfort or pain we have to endure, I strongly believe that it is better to face the challenges of acceptance as opposed to giving up hope and dwelling in negativity. Even when acceptance is not smooth or easy, it is most often better than the alternative. As a friend of mine sanguinely puts it, "My accepting something doesn't mean I like it or enjoy it, but I know that my not accepting it makes matters worse for me." Another friend explains it even more simply: "Life is easier that way."

As we proceed to examine important keys and tools in practicing acceptance in all our affairs, we need first overcome what is likely the most formidable acceptance barrier: denial. The next chapter explains how to do that.

CHAPTER FOUR

LETTING GO OF DENIAL

The worst lies are the lies
we tell ourselves.
—*Richard Bach, American writer*

VICTOR RESENTED HIS WIFE Janine's constant splurges on their eleven-year-old son, Kevin. In his words, "Janine buys him whatever he wants—video games, the latest tech and sports gear, expensive clothes—you name it. I keep asking her to stop, but she keeps doing it. She's spoiling Kevin rotten. I am at wit's end; I don't know what to do about it. I'm also bugged that she doesn't work and I'm paying for everything, but she gets all the credit."

When I suggested to Victor that perhaps he shouldn't give Janine so much money if she continues overindulging their son, he quipped, "I don't give her that much money. She uses a credit card—which I pay for too."

I then asked whether he felt he had any part in what was happening, and he quickly retorted, "No. What do you mean? Janine's the one who keeps buying Kevin everything—and I can't do anything about it!"

THE SIMPLE TRUTH ABOUT DENIAL

The irony of this domestic drama, of course, is that Victor keeps complaining to his wife while at the same time funding her extravagances. He was unable to acknowledge his role in the problem because he was in denial of the situation's underlying reality; namely, he was a primary cause of the indulgences because he kept funding them!

The simple truth is that you can't accept when you deny!

When we are in denial—whether it is something we did or didn't do, that someone else did or didn't do, or just the reality of a situation or circumstance that exists—we are not aware of that which needs to be accepted. Denial also includes wishful thinking, avoidance, self-righteousness, and turning a blind eye, to name just a few of its forms. Denial, for example, can come in the form of not dealing with a recurring health issue, avoiding coming to grips with a serious financial matter, or not accepting that your child has serious social problems. I once heard an apropos acronym for DENIAL: "Don't Even Notice I Am Lying."

The unfortunate paradox about denial is that it prevents us from making choices that could alleviate the very problems we are denying. Why? Because, we can't "see" them! Many of the stories in this book illustrate that once we are able to let go of denial, we can begin to address the important issues at hand, and beneficial new paths often emerge.

LETTING GO OF DENIAL

The transition from denial to awareness to acceptance is often a slow, arduous process, particularly when what we are denying or avoiding is painful. In such cases, there are rarely easy shortcuts.

In my personal experiences with denial, as well as observing others' struggles with it, I have noted some pertinent, related reasons behind it:

Our ignorance or unawareness of the underlying reality of a situation, or the "what is."

Our unwillingness to accept the "what is."

In short, you must be aware and willing. Unfortunately, it often takes the "pain and suffering" of living with denial before we begin to see the "light" of awareness and thereafter demonstrate the willingness and courage to act upon it.

These denial factors are prevalent in parents' trying to cope with the debilitating addictions of their children. Parents of children who are abusing drugs and alcohol, for example, are often reluctant to accept the seriousness of their children's addictive behavior. For many of them, it's easier to downplay matters or simply chalk things up to normal teenage and young adult antics. Other parents may be ignorant of the effects of drug and alcohol abuse and thus may see their children as being unmotivated or not trying hard enough at school rather than suffering from the consequences of excessive alcohol and drug use.

Denial can also take the form of a persistent belief that we have the power to change adverse circumstances.

Take the case of my friend Ken. A controller and problem solver by nature, Ken persisted in seeking a solution to his wife Jan's heavy drinking. He first tried reasoning with her, pointing out how her excesses were severely impacting their children as well as their own relationship. He also pointed to studies and statistics that demonstrated the high early mortality rate of heavy drinkers. Jan listened but didn't lessen her drinking. Ken next emptied wine and liquor bottles in their home, figuring if there was no alcohol in the house, Jan at least wouldn't be able to drink there. This failed, too, because she just purchased replacements—and hid them better.

Ken then pleaded with Jan to join Alcoholics Anonymous to get some help. That didn't work either because she denied she was an alcoholic. Finally, Ken threatened to leave her if she didn't stop drinking. This only made Jan go on more drinking binges.

At wit's end, Ken saw a therapist and shared with him the agonizing history of Jan's drinking woes and his persistent, but failed, efforts to get her to stop. A turning point came after a revealing dialogue with the therapist, which he shared with me:

KEN: What's particularly disheartening to me is that Jan's in total denial of her severe drinking problem.
THERAPIST: What about you?
KEN: What do you mean what about me?
THERAPIST: Aren't you in denial yourself?
KEN: Me? Of what?
THERAPIST: Well, aren't you in denial about how unmanageable *your* life has become as a consequence of your obsession with trying to find a solution to a problem that you are powerless to solve?

Ken was stunned by what the therapist had suggested, but he soon recognized the core truth about what had been revealed to him. He was so obsessed with trying to get Jan to stop drinking that he wasn't aware of how out of control his own life had become.

Ken's therapist recommended that he attend some Al-Anon meetings of a 12-step program for people like Ken whose lives had been impacted by friends or family with drinking problems. He was reluctant to go to such meetings at first—after all, he wasn't the one who had a drinking problem. However, after attending some meetings and listening to the experiences, hope, and insights of other attendees, Ken learned how important it was to keep the focus on himself and what he could do to improve his own shortcomings.

Al-Anon's First Step in particular resonated with him about his being in such denial: "We admitted we were powerless over alcohol and our lives had become unmanageable."

Ken later shared with me that when he finally accepted these undeniable facts, there was immediate relief: "It was as if a huge weight was lifted from my shoulders. I stopped trying to get Jan to quit drinking and began accepting her for who she was—a loving, caring person who was in the throes of a debilitating disease. Amazingly, I began to have more and more serenity in my life, despite her continued drinking. And two years later, Jan—on her own accord—joined AA and found sobriety."

Still another reason for denial may be the most challenging one to overcome: *our fear of embracing the underlying reality.*

Fear-based denial frequently presents itself when we are coping with serious health conditions. While denial can initially be helpful with the diagnosis of serious health conditions and diseases because it allows the person to process disturbing information while continuing in the usual activities of living, as the symptoms worsen, there needs to be a reassessment or "coming to grips" with what is happening. Overcoming initial denial thus becomes the necessary next step for returning to a healthy perception of the situation. With Parkinson's disease, for example, acceptance acknowledges the truth and reality of the diagnosis and initiates realistic expectations about its treatment and prognosis. It allows the person with Parkinson's to make reasonable and realistic plans for the future and allows family members to make appropriate adjustments.[1]

In such situations, it takes nothing short of great courage to overcome great fear and embrace the "new normal." However, as was the case with Chris and Karl in chapter 2, and others you will read about later, there is often a silver lining in moving from denial to acceptance. It allows you to better adapt to what you can realistically do, which not only reduces stress and anxiety, but also makes life more manageable.

MOVING FROM DENIAL TO ACCEPTANCE

Moving from denial to acceptance often entails being open to reexamining deeply ingrained beliefs, so that we can attain greater awareness of when, how, and what we are denying.

DENIAL SELF-INQUIRIES

Certain self-inquiries can help us gain the awareness necessary to let go of denial. Here are some pertinent ones:

> *Am I feeling anxious or fearful or angry about something or someone? If so, what?*
>
> *Is an important area of my life becoming unmanageable? If so, why?*
>
> *Do I play some part in what's troubling me, and if so, what is it?*
>
> *Am I avoiding dealing with something, and if so, what?*
>
> *Are my important relationships being impacted by something? If so, what is it?*
>
> *Am I engaging in wishful thinking about something important?*
>
> *Am I procrastinating about something, and if so, what?*
>
> *Am I being truly honest with myself about someone or some matter?*

I encourage you to reformulate and add to the above self-inquiries in a manner that will allow you to quickly get to the heart of any denial issues you may be experiencing.

Ultimately, you will find that letting go of denial is a gradual process of "awakening," involving a "to-and-fro" between the forces of denial and awareness. Know that as you continue to make headway, the gifts of acceptance will shine more brightly on you—even more so as you use the acceptance guide in the next chapter.

CHAPTER FIVE

THE SERENITY PRAYER: AN ACCEPTANCE GUIDE

> God grant me the serenity to accept
> the things I cannot change,
> Courage to change the things I can,
> And the wisdom to know the difference.
> > —*The Serenity Prayer, attributed to*
> > *Reinhold Niebuhr, 1892–1971*

THE FIRST THING I do upon awakening in the morning is get on my knees by my bed and recite the Serenity Prayer. It is a prayer for acceptance that enables me to be more fully aware, from the very start of my day, of the vast number of things I cannot control or change, and it reminds me that my very serenity depends on my willingness to accept them as they are. I find that the prayer works best when I apply its poetic phrases to the specific situations, circumstances, and people that are foremost in my life.

The keys and tools for fostering acceptance in this book are all enhanced by the guidance of the prayer.

Let's take a look at how we can apply the prayer's key elements in our lives.

ACCEPTING WHAT CANNOT BE CHANGED

I think that, like many people, I get stressed over relatively small matters. For example, one day I hit heavy freeway traffic on my way to a tennis lesson in Pasadena. I left my home early enough, but unexpected gridlock made it clear to me that I was going to be late for the lesson. I started to stress. What should I do? Should I call the instructor and let her know I'm running late? Good idea, except I didn't have her number with me. Should I get off the freeway and try surface streets? Maybe. But that might take even longer. Needless to say, my mind was soon spiraling at warp speed. I am embarrassed to admit that I even considered entering the carpool lane and risking a $400 ticket to make up for lost time!

Fortunately, I didn't. I finally caught myself and repeated that ever-important mantra, "I need to accept what is." I was in a situation that I could not change and I needed to somehow accept that. I focused on the underlying realities of the situation:

First—the traffic was very likely not going to ease.
Second—I was going to be late for the lesson.
Third—it would not be the end of the world.

This last thought settled me considerably by putting things in proper perspective. I realized that

One—I could turn on the radio and listen to some pleasing music.

THE SERENITY PRAYER: AN ACCEPTANCE GUIDE | 51

Two—I should be grateful that I had a safe and comfortable car in which to drive.

Three—even though I would be late, I would still have a lesson—just a shorter one.

My stress quickly dissipated, and if I didn't quite enjoy the remainder of the ride, I certainly didn't abhor it either! As it turned out, traffic abated after a few miles and I ended up being only five minutes late for the lesson.

This, of course, is a story about stressing over something that in the scheme of things is not that important. I call them "little stressors," but even those can easily mount over the day—and our stress level as well—if we don't come to some acceptance of our inability to alter them. It is of course even more debilitating when we deal with truly high-stakes matters. Whatever their importance, it helps considerably to be specific in identifying the factual basis or underlying reality, as I did with my freeway traffic jam. Doing so alleviates our stress and anxiety because things feel more manageable as our options become clearer to us.

There is a broad array of events and circumstances we clearly cannot change or control: internet and computer glitches, power outages, plane delays, and bureaucratic inefficiencies, to name a few. But even I, a controller, was usually able to accept such occurrences without much aggravation because I was *absolutely* sure that there was nothing I could do about them. Where I ran afoul was with those events and circumstances in which I felt there was a small chance—even a minute one—that I could alter the outcome. Ever the problem solver, my controlling head would rear up and I would lose what serenity I had at the time. It might, for example, be a business transaction that I pressed to complete before an unrealistic deadline, or waiting in line at the supermarket behind someone who took forever to sort through coupons. In those moments, acceptance certainly was not at the forefront of my thoughts!

We also cannot fundamentally change others, including our loved ones, family, and friends. Any changes must come from them, if they so choose or are able. Not accepting this truth impacts our serenity.

Many times, however, we have to deal with gray, untested areas in many aspects of our lives. That, coupled with the fact that life's natural currents are constantly moving and changing, can easily result in uncertainty—and even confusion—as to whether we can change or influence things. Why not then test the waters?

TESTING THE WATERS

If you are unsure about something or someone—meaning whether you can influence or change it or him—you can try being assertive or influencing events for a while to see how things go. When I do this, if at some time I feel uneasy or conflicted, I pretty much know it is then better to accept the situation or person as it is or he is and move on. An example is my having repeatedly urged one of my daughters to join Toastmasters because I felt it would give her confidence to speak in front of people, only to finally get a "Leave me alone, Daddy."

With practice and experience, I find that my acceptance threshold has moved forward considerably, as I believe it will for you as well. You become more aware of resistance, discord, and such when you are pressing or resisting too much. It is an ongoing, self-education process. Generally speaking, in cases of doubt I choose to accept rather than resist.

Ultimately, however, for me—and for many others I know—the solution lies in a journey of self-discovery as we seek the wisdom to know the difference.

THE WISDOM TO KNOW THE DIFFERENCE

I wish I could tell you the "wisdom to know the difference" comes easily. It usually doesn't. It would be simple indeed if we could readily distinguish between what we do and do not have the power to change or control. In truth, however, the distinction is frequently difficult. Strong emotions—fear and anger, for example—as well as high expectations easily thwart our intentions to realistically consider whether the issue is something over which we truly have power. Moreover, the line between wishful thinking (that we can change or control something or someone) and reality is often blurred. On other occasions, we may be able to influence things up to a certain point, and then we need to be wise enough to accept that's all we can do and move on.

THE PAINS OF BECOMING WISER

For many, the requisite wisdom comes only after enduring the hard, painful consequences of non-acceptance. One telling instance for me was the all-consuming legal battle I had with a former business partner, who I felt betrayed me in my weakest moment. The specific facts are not important, and I doubt that I could fairly recount them today, so enraged was I at the time. I literally felt like a lamb being led to slaughter, and that propelled me to fight and resist and to control at all costs, including my health. Even ending up in the hospital and enduring six major surgeries didn't cause me to relent.

Indeed, I tried everything—*except* to accept this person for who he was—a manipulative, cunning, and deceitful person. Shortly before trial, my attorney asked me what I wanted out of the case—meaning financially. I righteously announced to him my intention to make my partner stop taking advantage of people and change his unscrupulous business practices. Dumbfounded, my attorney turned to me and exclaimed, "Danny, you must be kidding! Do you really think you're going to change this man? That's just not going to happen."

The pains of nonacceptance will likely occur at different times and in varying degrees for each of us because there will always be things and people we aren't able to accept—at least initially. However, the frequency and degree of our discomfort can be reduced markedly as we learn to evaluate situations more realistically and with more patience.

STRATEGIES FOR AVOIDING THE PAIN

A question you might now be asking is, How can I accept, rather than persist or resist? Some strategies that will help you include

Pause and Reflect. When first faced with contentious issues or people, take a moment (or as some say, "pause") to consider whether you can realistically expect to change matters. Try not to react impulsively or retaliate. Fear and anger often emerge, and it is important to constructively process these emotions as soon as you are able (more on this later). The more grounded you are, the better you will be able to evaluate what is really at stake and its importance, and that will allow you to address the situation or person in a more constructive, responsive manner.

Ask Whether You Can Meaningfully Impact the Situation. Even if you feel you can change or have some impact on the matter or person, consider whether any success is worth the cost and energy—and anguish. In the case with my partner, it clearly wasn't. And I believe you will find that to be the case in many situations. What I have found extremely helpful is to ask myself, Can I have any *meaningful* impact on the person or situation? If I don't think I can, I accept the current situation or circumstance and move on. Similarly, it also helps to ask oneself questions such as How important is this to me? Is this something that is best left alone for now? Am I making a mountain out of a molehill?

Remember, not everything is a crisis, but anything can become one if you fail to let go of control and accept "what is."

Surrender to the Flow. Sometimes it is better to surrender than to win. That does not mean you have given up or were submissive; rather, it means you likely overcame a wounded ego, accepted "what is," and devoted your energies to more positive things. Another way of looking at it is to consider whether you would rather be right or be happy.

Consider, too, that what you may think is best for you often isn't; it may be something totally different from what you thought. I'm sure you've had situations where you didn't or couldn't get what you wanted or expected, only to have alternate avenues or opportunities open up later that were totally unexpected. That is because when we let go we are surrendering to the natural flow—and mystery—of life.

I have found time and again that by letting go and surrendering, I am able to glide intuitively and expansively within life's natural currents to destinations that have brought me greater joy, contentment, and achievements than I ever imagined possible. I sincerely believe it will be the same for you.

I had the chance to apply these strategies in connection with a real estate investment in which the lead investor unilaterally changed the terms of our agreement to benefit himself financially. I was particularly upset because it was presented to me as a fait accompli. In fact, at first I almost withdrew from the investment on the spot. However, having learned from the harmful consequences of my earlier impulsive conduct, I elected to step back and reflect on the matter for the next few days. In doing so I realized that my strong emotions prevented me from seeing three important truths. One, I was powerless to change my partner's decision since I owned a minority interest in the investment. Two, some of the changes would benefit me as well—something I clearly had overlooked in my anger. Finally, the business opportunity was still very advantageous for me in its altered format. I then "surrendered" to the situation and accepted "what was." In other words, I based my decision on facts rather than on emotions. To my surprise, my partner later reversed his decision and returned to the terms of the original agreement—something that would have never happened had I forced his hand.

Turn It Over to a Higher Power. "The wisdom to know the difference" is also frequently revealed through prayer and meditation. We can pray to God, a Divine Presence, or a Higher Power for the wisdom and guidance to make the right decision—for us. Similarly, we can meditate to clear our minds so that we can examine issues more calmly and objectively. Through such means, we gain clarity and perspective on troublesome issues, particularly where there is a fine line between what we can and cannot control, and we can better understand the likely consequences of our actions.

It can be extremely difficult when we reach the point where we know we are powerless over a person or situation and need to accept it and move on. We are only human, after all, and we are never free from the perennial conflict between what we *know* to be true and how we *feel* about it. We may not trust that things will work out if we leave well enough alone, or perhaps we fear that others might harm us. If you are having particular difficulty with this dilemma, the 12-step programs' concept of a Higher Power can be of considerable comfort. If we can come to believe that there is (or may be) a power greater than ourselves— be it a divine presence or God, as we understand him (or her), nature, love, or a transcendent energy force beyond our knowledge or capacity to understand—we can then turn over to this Higher Power the things with which we are struggling, including our doubts and uncertainties. A shorthand slogan for this is "Let go and let God."

The concept of a Higher Power is very personal and individual and is often based on our own experiences, epiphanies, insights, and wonderments. For many, it is also based on religious beliefs. However, we need not be religious or follow an established religion in order to believe in a Higher Power. The idea of a Higher Power can be tailored to meet our personal comfort and acceptance level. We need only accept that there is a force, or something, that is greater than ourselves—that we are not omnipotent or omniscient. (I once heard someone say to a doubter, "Do you believe you are the greatest power in the world?") The essential point is that if you are able to turn the things you cannot control over to something greater than yourself, then it is out of your hands, so to speak, and resistance to acceptance diminishes considerably, along with your obsessions and anxieties. You literally feel the burden lifted from your shoulders.

While there is an abundance of things and people in life that we cannot change, there are many things that are within our power to change or do. We can change our attitudes and deeply ingrained ways of thinking and doing things, for example. We can change the ways we respond to the displeasing actions of others and things. We need not be impulsive or overreactive. Instead, we can strive to be more humble and open-minded—and compassionate.

A good friend shared this insight on the subject:

"I realized that what brings me grief and deprives me of my serenity are not so much the troublesome or 'bad' things themselves, but rather how I react and respond to them."

Further, in almost all challenging situations, there will be choices and options that we do have. Most will require us to make changes in what we want or assert ourselves in ways that may feel uncomfortable or uncertain. It might be in the form of no longer coming to the rescue of a loved one, discontinuing a business that has stagnated, or telling a troubled and destructive child she is no longer welcome in our home. Reluctance and resistance to such changes and actions—whether because of guilt, shame, resentment, or other reasons—is natural and to be expected. However, such resistance can be overcome with willingness and courage.

In short, we can be guided by the second line of the Serenity Prayer by having the "courage to change the things I *can*."

USING THE SERENITY PRAYER AS A GUIDE

For some, applying the Serenity Prayer in their daily lives may feel foreign or even simplistic. I encourage you to be open to at least trying, perhaps with unimportant matters in the beginning. I find that it is very soothing to just state the words aloud. It takes the edge off things for me, and I don't think I'm alone in that. I am confident that as you begin feeling the comfort and serenity that comes with accepting the things you cannot change, you will find that the Serenity Prayer is a highly effective and practical guide to acceptance, particularly during times of great struggles and challenges.

ACCEPTANCE INTENTIONS

At the end of most chapters, I suggest some acceptance intentions applicable to their subject matter. These are aimed at making practicing acceptance easier and more effective for you. You can use them or modify them as you see fit. Here are some intentions that can be helpful in applying the Serenity Prayer.

With respect to the Serenity Prayer, I will

Repeat it each morning and several times during the day.

Apply it as specifically as I can to the situations and people that concern me.

Try to become more aware of what I cannot meaningfully change.

Surrender when I feel overly stressed.

Focus on what I have the power to change.

Pray for the courage to change those things.

Seek guidance from a Divine Presence or source in my life when I am uncertain what to do.

With a better understanding of the meaning of acceptance and its important benefits, as well as the guidance provided by the Serenity Prayer, let's next look at how we can better practice acceptance in important relationships in our lives—including those that constantly challenge us.

PART II

ACCEPTING OTHERS AS THEY ARE

CHAPTER SIX

ACCEPTING OUR LOVED ONES

The beginning of love is to let those we love be
perfectly themselves, and not to twist them to
fit our own image. Otherwise we love only the
reflection of ourselves we find in them.
—*Thomas Merton*, No Man Is an Island[1]

THE NORTH AMERICAN PORCUPINE has a real dilemma in accepting its mate, given that it has thirty
thousand quills attached to its body. In an article in
the *Travelers Rest Tribune,* columnist John Burns describes the formidable challenge that these animals
face: "They stand on their hind-feet and touch paws
in the so-called 'dance of the porcupines.' They pull in
their quills, accept each other 'as is,' and then begin a
close relationship."[2]

This is a good metaphor for our close relationships.
While we humans don't have to traverse such sharp obstacles, for most of us, these unpredictable and often
frantic times make intimate, supportive bonds with our
loved ones more challenging than ever. We need such

bonds to provide us with emotional anchors when dealing with stress and anxiety, as well as sharing the joy and wonders that are all around us.

Accepting our loved ones as they are is paramount to achieving love and intimacy. Not accepting them—quirks, idiosyncrasies, annoying habits, and all—severely hampers the love flow. We are in effect telling them that they are not good enough, that they fall short. And who wants to feel that way—particularly in matters of the heart?

Yet many of us constantly try to change the annoying traits and habits of loved ones or opine and advise what they should do differently and how they can "improve" their lives. We often don't support their personal choices. We also form unreasonable expectations of our loved ones and the relationship itself. In consequence, our loved ones are pressured to be other than who they really are (and wish to be) and don't feel they are accepted as they are. To no real surprise, dissension and resentment result, thereby obstructing the very things that are needed for intimacy and soulful connection—trust, understanding, and acceptance.

If porcupines manage to find ways to "accept" their "loved" ones, quills and all, shouldn't we be able to as well? Some practices and mind-sets that will go a long way toward achieving that follow.

KEYS TO ACCEPTING OUR LOVED ONES

There are a number of proven keys to accepting our loved ones.

MODERATE YOUR EXPECTATIONS OF YOUR LOVED ONE

Margaret, a visitor to my blog, shared how high expectations can hurt our love lives:

"Expectations have ruined countless intimate relationships I have had. I start out being fun and easygoing, but once the relationship begins to build, I start to expect a certain level of communication, contact and time together. . . . I almost don't know I'm doing it. I hear the person say they feel pressure and like everything has to be scheduled, yet I continue. It is horrible and not the way I want to be. I understand I need to let go, I just don't seem to know how to do it."

Margaret's quandary, unfortunately, is not uncommon. Many people I know have expressed similar regrets, and the common thread is almost always unreasonable expectations of their loved ones and relationships. I, too, have been prone to this pitfall—having few expectations at the beginning when the "love stakes" are low but steadily increasing as the relationship becomes more serious.

One thing I am now clear about, however:

When you expect too much of your loved one, you aren't accepting him.

It's not just with our loved ones. We will see later how unreasonable expectations also obstruct acceptance of our children, our parents, and our family, as well as our friends—even our foes! It plants the seeds of frustration and disappointment. Whether assertive or subtle, expecting too much of others pressures them to act and be as we want them to. It's also a double-edged sword. We are disappointed and resentful when our expectations are not met, and others feel the same when we do not accept them as they are.

Underlying many of our expectations are the needs we look to have fulfilled. For example, we may believe if the other person would be more nurturing or spend more time with us—instead of working so much or doing other things—we would be more content and less lonely. Or if she took more interest in our endeavors and passions, she would be giving us the love we need.

However, this belief system warrants scrutiny. Are we truly better off if others do as we want or expect? Is our happiness and well-being that dependent on others? I suggest not. When our focus and reliance is too much on others, we lose sight of what *we* can do to make things better for *ourselves*. We thus risk stymying our own growth and development.

In short, we give up our power to make our lives better.

Moreover, it is important to consider whether our needs are something that our loved ones can realistically fulfill. Most often they are something that only *we* can. There are several pertinent questions we can ask ourselves that will key us into whether we expect the wrong things from our loved ones.

Are there any unfulfilled needs of mine underlying my expectations of my loved one?
Am I looking for him to fulfill those needs?
Can he realistically fulfill those needs—even if he wanted to?

Another (and related) reason why we have high expectations of our loved ones is our need to change them. We feel *we* and/or *they* would be better off, even when we are hard-pressed to specify exactly how. It's more often the case that we don't know what's best for ourselves, let alone others! We thus need to let go of trying to change others if we wish to moderate our high expectations. That's why it is important to ask yourself,

Do I really have the power to change my loved one?

In most cases, we don't. The simple truth is that people will change when and if *they* choose or are able to do so, not because we want them to or feel it would be better for them. Making the above inquiry allows you to pause and consider whether you are effectively powerless over changing your loved one with respect to the personality trait or issue at hand. If you are, it is much easier to remove your expectations—and just accept the other person as she is.

There are two other pertinent questions we should ask ourselves.

Are my expectations of my loved one that important in the overall scheme of things?

Usually not! They may seem important at the time, but not when we take a moment to calmly reflect upon them.

Are my expectations placing undue pressure on my loved one?

Almost always! Indeed, pressure is a natural consequence of high expectations. Just think about the pressure and unease you feel when your loved one expects too much of you. Does that draw you closer to him? Consider this: while you may believe that your expectations will bring you and your loved one closer together, it is more likely that they will have just the opposite effect.

Consequently, it is only by reducing our expectations and demands of our loved one that trust and intimacy can blossom in "the space between."

FOCUS ON WHAT YOU LIKE ABOUT YOUR LOVED ONES

Accepting our loved ones as they are is fostered by focusing on the things we like and admire about them: sense of humor, sound moral values, a caring parent, a kind heart. Also think about all the nice things they regularly do for you: cooking nice meals, caring for you when you're sick, listening to your concerns, helping take care of your elderly parents.

Remember what originally attracted you to them. Their fun-loving, adventuresome, or easygoing nature. And keep in mind the good times you enjoy together. In short, focus on the *good* in them and the *good* they bring to your life. Doing these things will give you a more balanced perspective of your loved ones and their importance to you.

And remember,

No one is perfect and without flaws, least of all ourselves.

ADDRESS YOUR CORE ISSUES

Have you ever considered the possibility that your difficulty in accepting your loved ones has more to do with you than it does with them? It's likely more often the case than you might think.

My European friend Charles's difficulty in accepting Lydia is a case in point. From the start, sparks flew between them. Their sexual chemistry was off the charts. However, after the "honeymoon" period waned, their love connection was regularly derailed by arguments culminating in Charles's angry eruptions.

The dynamic went something like this: Lydia was sometimes unclear or noncommittal about what she wanted to do with Charles, such as taking trips together, and she would send mixed signals. Charles would pressure her to be clearer about what she wanted to do, usually to no avail. He would feel hurt and rejected by her evasiveness and then spew some harsh words, to which Lydia would respond in kind. Then all hell would break loose.

Their relationship could best be described as "Love and War."

Charles shared with me that he truly loved Lydia but felt so battered by their ongoing battles. Yet he was committed to finding ways to make things work between them. When we spoke again later on, he told me that their relationship had improved and they were having fewer arguments. When I asked him how this all came about, he replied:

"I am much better at accepting Lydia's ambiguities, even though they still bother me. I have come to realize that I cannot change that part of her. That's who she is. But it's more than just that."

"How so?" I asked.

"I did a lot of soul searching and was forced to face some hard truths," Charles replied. "I have always had unresolved abandonment issues stemming from early childhood traumas. I realized that's what made me try to control our relationship, pressuring her to do things with me when she wasn't sure if she wanted to. That, combined with Lydia's tendency to be unclear about what she wanted, was just lightning waiting to bolt."

"That makes sense, but was just simply becoming clear about those things enough?" I probed further.

"No, not really," Charles replied. "While it was very painful for me, I knew I had to find a way to overcome my childhood wounds if I wanted to defuse my anger and accept Lydia for how she was—which really and truly, was enough. In fact, I also realized I needed to change the way I was with almost *everyone!* I'm committed to doing the best I can—that's all I can do. I still have lapses, but as long as I continue to make progress, I am able to forgive myself. It's still all a work in progress and probably always will be. I will never be perfect and that's fine too."

As Charles's story illustrates, accepting our loved ones often requires identifying and overcoming our own shortcomings and core issues, whether they be fear of rejection and abandonment; loneliness; or feelings of not being attractive, good enough, or desired. When we don't address and process such feelings, they can easily lead to nonacceptance of our loved ones. We may, for example, misconstrue what they say or do, take matters too personally, or simply give them too much importance.

Once again, remember to ask yourself,

Is this more about me than them?

Many of us were drawn to our loved ones because of such attributes as their sense of adventure, fun-loving ways, charming personality, mutual interests, and personal accomplishments. But what happens with acceptance when your loved one has opposing views on important social and political issues?

RESPECT YOUR LOVED ONE'S CONTRARY VIEWS

Flash back to the 2016 presidential campaign and the politically divisive climate in which we all had our opinions and ideological stances. For many, that included their loved ones. But what if we vehemently disapprove of our loved one's political and social preferences and choices?

Consider these possibilities (or ones like them), for example:

What if you are a conservative Republican and she is a progressive Democrat?

What if you are for legalizing marijuana and he isn't?

What if you are pro-life and she is pro-choice?

What if you are for gun control and he supports the NRA?

I think you get the point—when loved ones so strongly disagree with each other, it's a real dilemma, one that could severely impair your love connection if you are not careful and thoughtful enough.

So what then can we do about this type of dilemma—short of having damaging arguments or parting ways?

One thing we *can* do is remember that our loved ones are individuals with their own feelings and leanings. While we may not agree with them, we must try to accept and love them for who they are and not who we want them to be. When we don't accept their right to their own views and preferences—even if these choices are repulsive to us—we communicate that they are not wise or informed enough and that their values are suspect. Are we not sending signals to them in our actions, gestures, and words that are meant to reconfigure them into another person altogether? This behavior is both destructive and selfish and is a powerfully hurtful approach to close relationships. Any changes must come from them, and the more we try to change or control them, the less likely it is that change will occur organically. Indeed, it aggravates an already sensitive subject, often causing them to dig in and hold to the selves they are most comfortable and confident with.

Secondly, we can remember what acceptance means—and what it doesn't—in such situations. It doesn't mean that you condone or agree with your loved ones' views and choices. Rather, it means that you accept their right to have them—*without judgment or resentment.*

Here are some instructive comments from readers of an article I wrote on the subject for a leading national blog:[3]

"I try to personify what I would like to see in others: a willingness to listen carefully, ask intelligent questions, and accept that I very well might be wrong and the other person may be totally right."

"One of my best friends and his wife share views on political and social issues that oppose mine. But our approach on touchy subjects has been to at least hear each other out and find common ground that we can agree on, even if it's a small thing. It's worked pretty well, and

I do actually respect their thoughts and opinions. It's definitely not easy having someone close to you believe in things you're against, so there has to be respect and awareness from both parties. Otherwise, it devolves into both sides fighting over ideas or one person going off on a topic while the other stays silent."

"I love my siblings and siblings-in-law, but all are on the other side of the fence. When we get together, I have learned to repeat 'no politics'"!

Finally, these wise words on acceptance by Thomas Merton found at the beginning of this chapter bear repeating:

"The beginning of love is to let those we love be perfectly themselves, and not to twist them to fit our own image. Otherwise we love only the reflection of ourselves we find in them."

Don't Try to Control Loved Ones or the Relationship

Alan and Rhonda had a great courtship. They enjoyed doing the same things together, including hiking and being in nature. They also had similar cultural and artistic tastes and enjoyed the same foods. In short, they were quite compatible, rarely experiencing conflict.

Their compatibility suffered, however, when they began living together. Alan was always organized. At work, his desk was neat and his records and files kept up to date. It simply made him feel and function better. He was also that way at home, more of a minimalist really, disposing of more things than he collected. Rhonda was the opposite. She was a collector and found it extremely difficult to dispose of things, even if they weren't being used. Clutter thus piled up in different areas of the house.

As you might expect, clutter and disorder unsettled Alan considerably. He had a lot of trouble accepting how Rhonda "operated" around the house. To him, it was so impractical and inefficient—you couldn't find things when you needed them, and the household was unsightly. He repeatedly pled his case to Rhonda. She listened politely but little changed. Unbeknownst to Alan, Rhonda didn't like clutter either and constantly struggled with what to do about it. She periodically removed some of it, only to have it reappear later in another spot. Alan continued harping until Rhonda retorted, "I don't have time to organize and sift through everything. You try taking care of the kids, doing the shopping and cooking, the laundry. . . ."

The end result was that Alan became enmeshed in turmoil by not accepting Rhonda for how she was and recognizing that it was beyond his power to change her, unless (and until) she wanted and was willing or able to change. His controlling efforts were doomed to fail.

As time went on, however, Alan found some constructive ways to lessen his discomfort. He considered what adjustments could be made to accommodate both their needs. He suggested maintaining certain clutter-free areas around the house so that he could retreat to them when he desired. Rhonda agreed. She even admitted that she really didn't like not knowing where things were herself, and this would be a good start for her to get better organized.

More importantly, on an internal level, Alan was able to get in touch with why he was so impacted by disorder. Like Charles, he tried to ascertain what core emotions were stirred up for him and what needs of his were unfulfilled. In doing so, he realized that as a child, keeping his bedroom neat and organized served as a kind of "safety valve" from the anxiety he experienced from being raised by an overbearing father and unprotective mother. This was a profound awakening for Alan and one that significantly diminished his discomfort around clutter.

As Alan's story teaches, our controlling actions prevent us from accepting our loved ones. I call this *love control*. Love control runs the gamut from unsolicited advice and opinions or criticism and judgment to unreasonable demands and expectations. It can also be subtle and seemingly unobtrusive, such as suggesting more than once that loved ones do something that we think will help them, or regularly coming to their rescue, or doing things that our partners should do for themselves.

The first step in letting go of love control and accepting your loved ones as they are is the awareness that you are a love controller or have the propensity to be one. Yet if you were to ask a loved one if she considered herself a love controller, my guess is that she would likely say no. Perhaps you would say no as well.

TAKE THE LOVE CONTROL TEST

Are you a love controller? Let's find out. Ask yourself the following with respect to your loved one:

Do I usually feel I know what's best for my partner?
Do I charm or pout or withdraw to get my way?

Am I often impatient with him?
Do I try to solve her problems?
Am I quick to point out my partner's shortcomings?
Do I expect my mate to act in certain ways?
Do I look to him for my own happiness?
Am I overly concerned that my loved one will not be able to resolve her personal issues?
Am I judgmental of him (be honest now!)?

"Yes" answers to these questions indicate you are trying to control the relationship. Now answer these questions:

Do I listen attentively to my loved one's concerns without trying to solve them?
Am I patient with her struggles?
Do I usually play a part in our love conflicts?
Do I accept my loved one's annoying habits?
Do I accept that my loved one is best suited to make the decisions that impact his life?

"Yes" answers to these questions indicate that you are not trying to control the relationship.

HONOR YOUR LOVED ONE'S CHOICES

All people, including our loved ones, have their own life path and are entitled to make the choices and decisions that influence and ultimately determine that path. We can have compassion for our loved ones and sincerely and lovingly want what's best for them, but we cannot truly *know* what is best for them—because we are not they. We look at things through our own history and filters, not theirs. Hence, we need to accept their choices, unless we or others are harmed by them. When we don't—whether by complaining, pressuring, or other methods of control—we aren't accepting them as they are, and we risk impeding and jeopardizing their path.

To be sure, none of this is easy. I have learned that I need to be more aware of my controlling inclinations and keep my ego in check or quiet that "I know what's best" part of me. I also need to remind myself that others' points of view and choices have validity—for *them*. The hard truth is that we are not nearly as omniscient or omnipotent as we are prone to believe, and the more we accept that, the more easily we can accept our loved ones—and others, as well.

Interestingly, on more than a few occasions, I have found that when I minded my own business and didn't pressure my loved ones to change their ways, they ended up changing them on their own. It may be that they were not yet ready or able to make the changes at first. It may also be that without demands or pressure, they could more objectively evaluate what wasn't working for them and make appropriate changes.

In the final analysis, accepting your partner for who, what, and how she is, is a choice that each of us has to make. We are essentially powerless over changing others' traits that we dislike, and trying to do so makes things worse. We are much better served by focusing on what we do have control over: our role in the relationship. Specifically, that includes our attitudes, our actions and reactions, our willingness to own up to our own shortcomings and part in relationship dysfunctions, and being humble and grateful for the love and support that others give us.

LOVED ONES ACCEPTANCE INTENTIONS

Today, with respect to my loved ones, I will:

Accept their personal choices.
See the "good" in them.
Moderate my expectations of them.
Remember there is more than one "right" way.
Not judge or criticize them.
Not pressure them.
Live and let live.
Be grateful for all the nice things they do for me.

As we try to implement these intentions, it is helpful to remember that our loved ones—like ourselves—are people with their own histories and are seeking their own paths to fulfillment, and honoring that is a demonstration of our love for them.

To a great extent, the keys to accepting our significant other are the same as for accepting other people in our life—particularly our children, as we will see in the next chapter.

CHAPTER SEVEN

ACCEPTING OUR CHILDREN

Parents. If you teach us only to be like you, then
how do you expect us to live in the future?
—*Lana Miller, 6th Grade Graduation Speech*

EDA HAD FOND MEMORIES of participating in her
native Eastern European scouts group while growing
up in the Midwest. She always looked forward to the
two-week summer sleepaway camps in the peaceful
forests of Wisconsin, where she learned practical survival skills and her native country's cultural traditions
and folk songs. After her daughter Katarina was born,
Eda eagerly awaited the time when Katarina could also
participate in scouts' activities. Eda had high expectations that Katarina would enjoy the scouts as much as
she had. And as a youngster, Katarina did, when she
attended weekend summer minicamps with her mother.
However, as Katarina entered adolescence and began
attending ten-day sleepaway camps without her mother,

79

she felt out of place and excluded by the other girls because she didn't speak their native language.

When Katarina went to her mother and told her she wanted to drop out of scouts, Eda pressed her to continue, promising things would get better. Katarina relented and agreed to attend camp the following summer. Things didn't improve. She became adamant about not continuing in scouts. The two of them argued whenever the subject was raised, impairing their close bond.

After conferring with several close friends, Eda realized it was unfair to impose her desires on her daughter. She let Katrina know that she no longer had to continue in scouts. In short, Eda accepted that Katarina had the right to make her own decision in the matter.

Nine months later Katarina's path took an unexpected turn when, to her mother's surprise, she announced that she wanted to rejoin scouts and attend the upcoming summer's camp. And what happened was scarcely predictable: Katarina became close friends with some of the very campers who previously shunned her. Over the next five years, Katarina actively participated in scouts. She earned successive achievement awards (colored scarves) given by camp elders after she passed stringent tests. She was also selected to be on the scout leadership board that planned and supervised activities for the younger scouts.

Thus, by accepting her daughter's wishes, Eda was bestowed with even greater blessings than she had hoped for.

Like Eda, many parents pressure their children to follow the same paths they did or ones that they believe are "best" for their children. These parents have high expectations of their children, particularly with regard to educational and vocational decisions, as well as with sports and social activities. These highly controlling parents try to make their children something they aren't instead of accepting them for who they are. Considerable harm to children can easily result from parents' nonacceptance of them, including low esteem, as Hans's story relates.

Hans constantly felt degraded by his father's constant rejections of him as a child, as he shares:

"During my childhood, my father's expectations were unreasonable and I could not cope. We argued every day about something, and he could not accept me or anybody else. I had no self-confidence and low self-esteem because I never thought that I was good enough. Everything I did had to be perfect in order for me to feel good about myself, but this way of thinking actually caused me to reject myself. It was not until I later learned to accept myself that my self-esteem improved, which allowed me to accept others as well."

Recent studies confirm the significant harm of stringent parental demands on their children. Research from the University of New Hampshire found that authoritarian parents whose parenting style is summed up as "it's my way or the highway" are more likely to raise disrespectful, delinquent children than parents who listen to their children and gain their respect as legitimate authority figures.[1]

Similarly, in "Ambitious Parents, Mellow Children," *Wall Street Journal* columnist Sue Shellenbarger notes that type A parents have particular difficulty in accepting their type B children. Significant problems arise when such parents push their children too hard, pile on unreasonable demands, and criticize them when they are already doing their best.[2]

THE FUNDAMENTAL PARENTAL CHALLENGE

Parental acceptance and parental control are inextricably linked. When parents micromanage their children's lives, they are not accepting of them. Consequently, practicing parental acceptance in almost all cases requires that parents relinquish some amount of parental control. Yet in raising my three children, I observed that most parents are reluctant or perhaps afraid to give up much control or "authority." This quandary underpins what I call the "Fundamental Parental Challenge": ensuring their children's health, safety, and well-being; fostering good morals, family values, and ethics; and encouraging learning—while not obstructing their children's personal growth, self-reliance, and life path.

Parents must face this challenge every day—and at times it feels like every moment! It is always there. The line between the two is often murky. Consider, for example: When does doing too much for your children mean that we deprive them of valuable learning experiences? When does overly influencing their choice of classes or schools or friends mean that we don't accept and trust that they know what's best for *them?* When is the issue really about *us* and not *them?*

At what point are we controlling our children too much and not accepting them enough? These and similar issues should be determined by parents based on their particular circumstances and the individual nature of their children.

ACCEPTANCE GUIDELINES

Certain relevant guidelines in the form of self-queries can greatly assist in knowing when we are crossing the line from acceptance to overmanagement of our children's lives.

AM I BEING TOO CONTROLLING?

Mitchell Rosen, a licensed therapist, felt he knew what was best for his two children and didn't mind letting them know, even after they matured into young adults. Such parental "omniscience" is ingrained with control, and Mitchell struggled to let it go. He learned, however, that acceptance was the most effective way to temper his need to control his children. In his words:

"If our relationship is always predicated on 'Father Knows Best,' it will be too limited. Oh, don't get me wrong, I do think I know best, but I also understand he needs to make his own decisions no matter how misguided I may think of them.

"More and more it's happening that his decisions, the ones I thought were off the mark, turn out to be spot on. It is humbling but at the same time reassuring when I discover my son's (or daughter's) harebrained scheme turns out to be the wisest choice. I realize my purpose as a parent is to prepare my children to be independent . . .

"It's a process of *letting go* and *acceptance*. Accepting that my children may know more than me or that their lives truly belong to them requires me to let go. I doubt that I'll ever stop being opinionated but if I don't temper my insistence, I may eat Thanksgiving dinner alone."³

Like Mitchell, I was a major controller who felt he knew what was best for his children—and didn't hesitate to let them know. When my oldest child, Brandon, was young I constantly offered my "two bits" on almost everything he did, thinking it would help him better traverse life's many challenges. It also made me feel more a part of his life. It never occurred to me that it would be better to let him spread his wings by himself, even if that meant falling down at times.

Brandon had no choice but to put up with my intrusions when he was younger. In his teens, however, he became very dismissive of me—he didn't want to hear it anymore and let me know it. A very uncomfortable wedge grew between us.

Our relationship remained strained until I began accepting that he was the one who could make the best decisions for himself—not me. I also accepted that he was different from me in many ways and had his own ways of doing things. I thus no longer offered my unsolicited opinions and advice. Instead, I tried to listen attentively whenever *he* chose to offer information about his affairs.

When he later entered the "real" world after graduating college, he began opening up to me more about job issues and personal concerns he had. Sometimes he sought my input as well, and it was only then that I offered it. Our bond improved considerably and continues to this day, mainly because I accept him for the man that he is and the one best suited to make the decisions that impact his life.

Due to fear and concern for our children's well-being, many—maybe most—parents are too controlling. We feel we know what's best for our children. However, we run the risk of seriously impacting our bonds, as I did with Brandon. We should also always be cognizant that overmanagement of our children's lives risks jeopardizing their personal growth and development, their resiliency—and ultimately, their life paths.

A case in point concerned a friend who constantly intervened in his bright son's job and career decisions. He funded several of his son's failed business ventures in which he was the "chief advisor." The son became so reliant on his father's advice—and approval—that confidence in his own judgment suffered greatly and this ultimately impeded his career path.

DO I LISTEN ATTENTIVELY TO MY CHILDREN?

Listening attentively to our children is a very healing process that leads to acceptance—by our children, as well as ourselves. Listening attentively means "hearing" their desires and concerns *without* advising, judging, or criticizing. I refer to this as "due process" parenting, where parents engage in open dialogue with their children, considering their points of view and concerns and remaining open to reexamining or modifying their positions. It is important to give due consideration to the innate differences in life circumstances and cultural/societal environments between our childhood and our children's. Just think for a moment how different our parents' childhoods and our childhoods were. It is likely even more so today with respect to our own children.

This open-minded process not only promotes mutual trust and respect but also results in agreements and decisions that are more likely to be accepted and adhered to by our children.

WILL I OBSTRUCT MY CHILD'S LIFE PATH?

As a successful artist and executive in the film and entertainment industry, Miriam found it important that her daughter, Amber, be similarly trained in the creative arts. However, when she was a fifth grader, Amber began resisting her mother's "timetable" for her creative development. Taking note of her daughter's strong-willed nature, Miriam adjusted her wishes for what she wanted for Amber. She poignantly explains how accepting her daughter's different life path brought unexpected blessings:

"Amber has her own life journey and I don't want to take that away from her. She will do what she does in her own time. She was late in learning to crawl, and I was really concerned about that, so I tried all kinds of things to teach her how but was unsuccessful. Then I accepted I couldn't change the situation and stopped trying, and she started crawling two weeks later. The same thing occurred with her piano lessons. I wanted her to learn classical music, but she kept resisting. So I stopped giving her lessons. A few years later, after a voice lesson, she started playing a few chords on the piano, and before I knew it she was avidly learning to play to accompany her singing. The same thing happened at school. Amber was always a B student, and I fretted that she was not going to get into college. Then in eighth grade, on her own, she started studying more and got straight As.

"I am now very clear that my role is to love and care for her, support her, keep her as safe as I can, and let go of just about everything else. And what joy Amber gives me!"

But what if you believe your child is making really poor choices? Should you just stand by and accept them? Nathan's story below sheds some light on this frequent parental dilemma.

WILL MY NONACCEPTANCE STRAIN THE RELATIONSHIP?

Nathan and his daughter, Rachel, had a combative relationship ever since the time she was a young teenager. Nathan felt Rachel was too impulsive and that she exercised poor judgment regarding her social life and choice of friends. Fearful that she might go astray, he often felt compelled to put his foot down about her activities. However, Rachel was strong-willed and frequently rebelled, creating an undercurrent of anxiety and discomfort in their household. It finally reached the point where there was very little communication between the two.

When Rachel began college at eighteen and gained more independence, she started pulling away from her family. Wanting to maintain some semblance of a relationship with his daughter, Nathan loosened the reins and was more accepting of her choices—including her decision to drop out of college and date a man fifteen years her senior.

I asked Nathan how he was able to accept his daughter's choices. He replied:

"It really came down to the fact that I realized that I no longer could change the way she was or the choices she was making, short of cutting off ties with her altogether—and I knew for sure that's not what I wanted. So I just backed off and welcomed her boyfriend into our family."

"That must have been hard for you," I responded.

"It was," Nathan answered, "but it was made much easier by my realization that I really don't know what's best for her or what the future holds for her—or me, for that matter. Maybe her choices will turn out to be good ones for her. Who am I to say or know? It's a mystery to me, and one I certainly can't solve. A lot of things can happen, good and bad. When I think back on my own life, where I am today—and that's a pretty good place—it could not have been predicted by the choices I made at Rachel's age. Maybe she has to go through the suffering of making some bad personal decisions in order for her to fully develop into who God intended her to be."

As Nathan's story illustrates, accepting our children as they are often requires making soul-searching decisions. Do our children truly need our protection? Should we let them stumble? Do we want our children to remain a part of our lives, and if so, how much and in which ways? How will our decisions impact ourselves and the rest of the family?

In considering which decisions I should make regarding my children, I am governed by my belief that every child is unique, with his or her own nature, talents, and life journey, and my primary role as a parent is to accept and foster that. When we don't accept—or at least seriously consider—our children's desires and choices, we risk obstructing their personal growth and unique life paths. I believe it is up to our children to fulfill their own destinies. It is important to allow them the opportunity to make mistakes and learn from them. Parental acceptance fosters independence, self-sufficiency, resiliency—and self-esteem.

In that sense, acceptance is a true expression of our love.

My beliefs certainly didn't occur overnight. I first had to learn to be more humble.

Is My Way the Only or Best Way?

I always felt my youngest daughter, Lana, should adopt the same study habits that I found successful in school. To wit: take good class notes, study in a quiet room or area, sit up straight, and prepare well in advance for upcoming tests. Of course, as a controller by nature, I didn't hesitate to ask her to do the same— many times over.

To my chagrin, Lana continued to do things differently. She took very few notes, listened to loud music while studying, and usually studied while reclined in bed—and waited until the last minute before cramming for important tests. To say the least, I had trouble accepting her study habits. On one telling occasion, when she was twelve years old, I pressured her to begin studying for her finals well in advance of the test dates. Lana looked up at me and without missing a beat, responded:

"Daddy, I can't do it that way. I'm different from you and I process things differently. Listening to rock music helps me study better and I need a sense of urgency to concentrate."

I was immediately taken aback by my daughter's truth. Lana really is different from me—vastly so. She budgets her time differently, prioritizes differently, has different interests and talents, and has difficulty focusing for extended periods of time. There was one thing we had in common, though. She consistently received good grades.

Through our encounter, I was blessed with a very powerful acceptance insight: Who am I to say that my way is the best way—for her or anyone else? "My way" is just a way, nothing more. Just because it works well for me doesn't mean it will for others.

AM I BEING SMUG OR ARROGANT?

So-called parental "omniscience" is pervasive in raising our children. True, we've experienced much more in our lives—particularly hardship—than our children and concurrently have gained certain life wisdoms. But in truth, those wisdoms are mostly helpful to our own lives going forward and not necessarily our children's. On point, a friend once remarked about his children, "My solutions are often worse than their problems!" We should thus remind ourselves that what has worked well for us—and what hasn't—in our lives may not serve our children the same way. Everyone is unique and responds to events and challenges differently. To believe that our way is best for others—particularly our children—borders on arrogance. The sooner we recognize such limited thinking, the better we can accept our children's desires and choices and thereby foster their growth and independence, as Mitchell and Miriam did.

Being more humble has enabled me to accept my children as they are and thereby serve them best as a loving supporter, confidant, and at times, mentor and protector. In doing so, I am privileged to both enjoy and learn from their unique attributes and talents. They have been my teachers in many respects.

ARE MY DESIRES AND EXPECTATIONS REALISTIC?

Kimberly McCafferty wisely recognized the importance of separating her desires and expectations from those of her autistic son, Justin. When Justin was first diagnosed with autism, she strongly hoped he would eventually be able to live independently of her. She wanted him to be able to attend college, marry, and take care of his basic needs. As time went on, however, Kimberly realized that Justin would not be one of those children at the milder end of the autistic spectrum. Courageously, she was able to distinguish between her needs and her son's:

"I know I grieved for those choices he would never have, but even then I acknowledged that these were life choices I needed to be happy. My boy didn't."[4]

This realization helped her overcome her grief and move on to accepting Justin's probable life journey, one that would need constant support. In accepting that he would have to live with formidable limitations, she was able to realistically assess the practical things she could do to help him make his life more joyful, productive, and safe for him.

Like Kimberly, we need to remind ourselves that what we want or desire for our children may not be what's best for them or in alignment with their unique characters and natures. What makes us happy and content won't necessarily make our children happy and content. Parents in 12-step programs express this belief by acknowledging that their children have their own Higher Power—and it's not their parents!

Is My Ego Too Involved?

Sometimes our unwillingness to accept our children's desires and choices is motivated by our ego-based concerns, such as social standing, possible embarrassment, and concern about other parents' opinions of our parenting, rather than serving the higher needs of our children.

Thus it's important to keep our ego at bay as much as we can. We should ask ourselves whether our decision or demand is more about *us* than *them*. We should also take care not to make it a battle of the wills or struggle to prove we are right. While parental respect is certainly important, we need to be sure that our insistence for respect isn't used as justification for unfair demands.

To be clear, however, in recommending these acceptance guidelines, I am by no means endorsing permissive parenting where few rules and boundaries are set, but simply that parental oversight and control should be exercised in moderation. It should be used primarily for our children's health, safety, and social, moral and spiritual well-being. As mentioned before, the challenge for parents is finding the right balance between too much acceptance and control, with due consideration given to the unique character, nature and maturity of our children. Making these inquiries helps me considerably in reaching that balance for each of my three children, and the scales were different for each of them because each of them is different.

KAHLIL GIBRAN HAD IT RIGHT

These acceptance paradigms are not new. Kahlil Gibran encapsulated them long ago in his famous book *The Prophet*, when he wisely said that our children are not *really* our children and that though they come through us and are a part of us, they don't belong to us. While we should give them our love and thoughts, they have their own thoughts, and we should thus not try to make them like us.[5]

During her sixth-grade graduation ceremony, my daughter, Lana, in her own interpretation of Gibran, urged parents to be more accepting of her classmates. She said:

"Parents, if you teach us only to be like you, then how do you expect us to live in the future? Right now, we are figuring out who we are and who we will become. All you can do is give us love and support. Believe in us and we'll make the right choice."

Since that time I have tried to acknowledge her points of view and am still gratefully receiving the resulting gifts. Yet, lest there be any doubt about it, there will be times when the decision whether to accept our children's ways and choices can be excruciatingly difficult. That's when these acceptance guidelines are most helpful.

However, even when we successfully apply them, our prudent parental decisions can be subverted by perhaps what is the foremost obstacle to acceptance: fear.

OVERCOMING PARENTAL ACCEPTANCE FEARS

Perhaps no fears are as strong and pervasive as the ones we have regarding our children's well-being and happiness. We easily become preoccupied with the many "what ifs" and "what might happens" to our children, and consequently our perspective is clouded about what really is at stake in many aspects of their lives. We also lose sight of our children's ability to adequately—and safely—take care of their needs. Like I did with Lana, we may fear that if we accept the helter-skelter ways in which our children do their homework or study for important tests, they will falter at school. We may worry that they may not get into college (or at least not a good one) and hence not be able to land a good job upon graduation. Or perhaps we might fear that our child's ungainly appearance or behavior quirks will prevent him from finding a good life partner. If you are a parent, you know the list goes on and on!

Importantly, it is primarily such fears that make it so difficult for us to stop micromanaging our children's lives, moderate our expectations of them, be open-minded and listen to their needs, and ultimately honor their life paths.

It is thus paramount that parents address and process their fears in a timely and objective manner. It begins with being clear about what they are, then assessing their merit, and finally taking the appropriate action—or inaction—as the case may be. In the process, you will find that your parental fears often leave on their own accord—likely because they were speculative or illusory—much in the same way the defroster clears fogged car windows.

Here are some tools and strategies that will let you effectively process your parental fears—and for that matter, your fears about most things in life.

Specifically Identify Your Fears

If you want to process your fears, first, know clearly what they are. Many times they are not readily known to us, or known only generally. That's because fear often basks in our ignorance and is a master of disguise. We may attribute the anxiety or discomfort that we feel about accepting our children's choices to something other than fear—anger or exasperation, for example. Hence, we may deny or reject things our children want to do because it gives us some immediate relief to not have to deal with it. However, such relief is usually short-lived and displaced by longer lasting consequences—possibly losing the trust and willingness of our children to share their concerns with us.

One of the best ways to detect this most tricky of emotions is to do a *fear inquiry*. When you feel unsettled or anxious about your child, take a moment and think about what you might be afraid of. If it's a generalized feeling, push further. The answer might lie in the pit of your stomach or in a tightened chest or throat. You might ask yourself, Am I fearful of my child going astray? Not doing well in school? Using drugs? Harming herself? Choosing the "wrong" friends? Not being accepted by his peers? Not getting enough sleep? Taking on too much? And so on.

The key in all this is to expose our parental fears as soon as possible. Doing so immediately weakens their hold over us. The good news is that just exposing these fears to some "light" helps us to overcome them. Once our fears are unmasked, we feel less anxiety and we can then engage our children more calmly. We can reason things out with them, better listen to their concerns, and when necessary, set appropriate boundaries and limits.

CONFRONT YOUR ACCEPTANCE FEARS

Once you have a clearer understanding of your acceptance fears, the next step is to confront them. Move "closer" to them, if you will. I call this process "facing and embracing." This takes courage, for at this juncture the easiest thing for us is to deflect our fears. Stay with any discomfort caused by your fears, even for a short while. Sense them, feel them, "lean" into them—including physically—and accept that it is okay to feel discomfort. I can tell you with some confidence, however, that if you "lean" into your fears, their grip will loosen dramatically. The basis of most fears is more illusory than real. If you constantly remind yourself of this, your fears will not undermine you.

Don't, however, sulk or dwell on them; simply give them their just due. As you do, be cognizant that our feelings are not facts. Fears are just feelings and emotions, nothing more, nothing less.

SEPARATE FACTS FROM ILLUSIONS

Apt acronyms I have heard for FEAR are "*Future Events Already Ruined*" and "*False Evidence Appearing Real*." Think about this for a moment. Isn't it the case that most of our fears are based on suppositions, speculations, and assumptions concerning events that haven't yet occurred? Reflect back on your prior experiences—and, of course, your children's. More often than not, such dreaded future events probably never occurred, or at least not in the way we imagined.

Accordingly, take some time to separate the objective facts and truths of the underlying situations and circumstances concerning your children from the illusions and unfounded assumptions and speculations that your imagination has conjured up. For example, ask yourself: "How important is it in the overall scheme of things?" Much of the time it is not important. "Are my children equipped to handle the situation?" Most of the time they are. "Will any real harm come from it?" Usually not. And, "Am I depriving them of a valuable learning experience?"

The obvious takeaway from this is to do your best to remain in the moment with whatever truths are revealed to you. Deal with what is real *now*, not what might happen tomorrow. Any method or format that you choose is fine. Disregard all the "mights," "maybes," and "could bes" that only stir up your fears. Trust that you—and your child—will be able to handle whatever may happen tomorrow—and even more so when your focus is on handling what is before you today.

Empowering Our Children through Acceptance

Accepting our children allows them to be more fully themselves—without pressure or judgment—and thereby make the choices that are invariably best for *them*. It encourages them to explore and gain the independence and self-reliance that results from that. At the same time, they become more willing to open up and share their real concerns and struggles, and if we are able to simply "be there" for them at such moments, real bonding and healing occurs.

What greater gift can we—and they—have!

Acceptance Intentions for Parents

Today, with respect to my children, I will

Listen attentively to them.
Confront the fears I have regarding them.
Recognize that my way is not the only way.
Not try to solve their problems.
Moderate my expectations of them.
Trust that they will make the right decisions—for them.
Appreciate the good in them.
Understand that what works for me may not for them.
Recognize and respect our differences.

It's one thing for us to try to accept our children as they are. But what about the reverse? As adult children, how important is it that we try to accept our parents as they are, particularly if we believe they are responsible for our current struggles? And how can we better do that? The next chapter addresses those and other important questions.

CHAPTER EIGHT

ACCEPTING OUR PARENTS

Honor your father and your mother.
—*Book of Exodus 20:12*

"WHETHER YOU LIKE IT or not, Danny, we're stuck with each other." Those were the first words out of my father's mouth at a pow wow we had some fifteen years ago after a severe falling out that lasted six months. His statement rang true. To my father's credit, his cryptic words led to a candid discussion in which we hashed out our differences. Our relationship has since strengthened with each passing year, and my father and I now have a great deal of mutual respect and love for one another, precisely because we learned to accept each other more fully.

The fact is that there are certain inextricable emotional (and likely genetic) bonds in the parent-child relationship that make a complete severance of ties extremely difficult, if not near impossible. Even when parents and children don't see or talk to each other for long periods of time, there nonetheless remains emotional linkage—or "baggage"—between them that impacts their well-being.

This is not to say, however, that where there has been severe parental abuse (including emotional and sexual), violence, or similarly harmful behavior, that children should accept their parents at all costs. It is a very personal decision. Many who suffered severe parental abuse are adamant about not forgiving or accepting their parents, feeling that no benefit would be derived therefrom. Others, such as Iva in chapter 2, choose to forgive their parents as a means of letting go of resentment for a painful past and freeing them to move forward with their lives.

In any case, it is important to remember that acceptance does not mean that you are excusing or condoning your parents' behavior. Rather, for many children, it is a way to emotionally and spiritually detach themselves from the resentment that accompanies such behavior. For that reason, accepting our parents as they are at least warrants serious consideration.

Learning how others have come to accept their parents can be instructive because of the commonality of issues present in many parent-child relationships. Take Gene's story, for example.

Growing up on a small farm in a Midwestern town, Gene was always crushed by his father's constant criticisms and lack of acknowledgment. When he received Bs and B+s in his classes, his father wanted to know why he hadn't gotten As. When he had an off day on the playing field, his father harped on his lack of effort. In Gene's words, "Whatever I did was never good enough for him. I longed for the pat on the back, the 'great job,' the 'I'm proud of you, son.' But they never came. Only the criticisms."

As he witnessed warm expressions of love, including hugs and sometimes even kisses, between his friends and their fathers, Gene began to question whether his father loved him. His mother reassured him his father did, but it was of little consolation. When he later left home, his father was critical of his friends and lifestyle, but he had gained some independence and was no longer willing to put up with it. Constant clashes resulted between them. Gene describes it:

"When I started standing up to my dad, he felt disrespected and gave me the 'silent' treatment, sometimes not speaking to me for months on end. There was always that excruciating dead silence when we sat around the dinner table. I felt totally ignored and raged inside. My mother would become sick and depressed by it all and I always ended up having to apologize to him to end her downward spiral. The really crazy thing about it is that I actually believed this was a 'normal' father-son dynamic, until I later learned otherwise in therapy."

Their relationship began to improve years later after Gene learned that his father's own father was a truck driver who binged all the time and was never there for his family, causing his younger sister to go astray at an early age. At only fourteen years of age, his father awoke early before school started and drove a beaten-up old truck to make egg deliveries to the local markets to help his mother with household bills. At nineteen, he enlisted in the navy to serve in the Second World War after marrying, and was greeted by a three-year-old "stranger" upon his return.

Awareness of these things gave Gene a great deal of compassion for his father. He shares:

"My dad did the best he could as a father who was still coming of age. He simply didn't have the 'tools' to show me the love and affection I needed. He also didn't want me to end up like his sister, and that's why he was so hard on me.

"When he later underwent treatment for cancer, I took time off from work to drive him to his doctor appointments, which gave us time to get to know each other better. As I said goodbye to him after a particularly grueling day of medical procedures, his eyes teared up, he reached over to hug me, and whispered 'I love you, Gene.' That was all it took. The uncomfortable barrier between us was down forever."

There are other gifts that can come with accepting our parents. Acceptance can be very liberating, and more so with regard to our parents. It releases us from the shackles of the past and the anger and resentment for what they did or didn't do for us or give us. Even if our parents did cause serious issues for us, two things are certain: (a) blaming them will not change matters, and (b) we are the only ones who can overcome the hand we were dealt. In no longer being bound to our parents for our happiness and security, we are free to discover who we really are and who we can become.

> *Simply put, we have a choice: we can dwell on past parental transgressions and remain stuck in the past—or we can accept our parents as they are and be free!*

Still another gift is that it makes us better parents ourselves. When you feel the "void" of not having received love, understanding, and support from your parents and understand how it has impacted your life, you have a greater awareness of the importance of providing the same to your own children. Moreover, you are given the opportunity to do so. Hence, if your parents gave little consideration to your views and interests, you can give due consideration to those of your own children. Similarly, if there was little openness and communication with your parents, you can choose to be open and candid with your children. If your parents never "owned up" to their mistakes and transgressions, you can teach them the virtue of humility by owning up to yours.

While the opportunities to help and nurture our children are vast, we should take care to do so with moderation and balance, lest it have an impact opposite of what is intended. For instance, because my father was overly critical and strict with me, I tried to become too much of a friend to my own son and not enough of a father. There were times when consequences for Brandon's misbehavior were warranted—and would have benefited him—but I failed to provide such. I thus believe there should be some moderation with respect to complimenting and building up our children, particularly when it is not factually warranted. Otherwise, it could create an inflated sense of self and diminish their resiliency when they later deal with life's hard knocks.

KEYS TO ACCEPTING OUR PARENTS

If you choose or desire to try to accept your parents more fully, or honor them, there are certain practices and mind-sets that are helpful.

PROCESS YOUR NEGATIVE FEELINGS

Negative feelings toward our parents (anger, resentment, bitterness, and the like), no matter how well-founded, are formidable barriers to acceptance. They drive a strong wedge between parent and child. Even if the feelings are not overt, they still create the elephant in the room.

It is often the case that adult children are not fully in touch with their negative feelings toward their parents until after they have undergone counseling or therapy to deal with personal issues such as rage, loneliness, or feelings of unworthiness. As adult children become aware that many of their hardships are integrally related to their parents' "faults," it can stir up anger and resentment—and of course blame, with children seeking "apologies" for, or acknowledgments of, parental missteps. When the same are not received, the divisions are further exacerbated.

However well-founded, such negative feelings hurt mainly ourselves. As expressed earlier, we need to let go of our resentments and grudges related to past parental transgressions if we want to free ourselves to move forward with our lives. It thus clearly behooves us to find ways in which to "dissolve" any anger and resentment we are holding toward our parents. Being compassionate is one effective way.

BE COMPASSIONATE

Just as we do, our parents have shortcomings that are reflected in both their actions and omissions. Our parents may not have had opportunities such as therapy or counseling to improve upon their limitations. Also, parenting styles and norms have changed—I believe significantly—over the years. During my childhood (many moons ago!) parenting in general was much more disciplinarian and dictatorial and less democratic than it is today.

Consequently, like Gene, having compassion for our parents facilitates forgiveness and acceptance. Context is important. It helps to take into account what they went through as children—their struggles, degree of education, socioeconomic status, social norms at the time, and such—and how their own parents parented them.

I am reminded about what my father once told me after I had complained about his parenting: "Danny, we did the best we could." And he did. This is not to say that parents are justified in any harm they have caused their children, but rather it reminds us that our parents, like ourselves, are not perfect.

LOWER YOUR EXPECTATIONS

As previously noted, undue expectations of others is an obstacle to practicing acceptance and no less true with our parents. In fact, the expectations we have of our parents are frequently greater than those we have for anyone else. We look to them to be our caregivers, our nurturers, our protectors—and our role models. Yet, as in some of the stories shared in this book, our high expectations pressure our parents to be and do other than how they are and feel. This can easily create not only resentment on their part but also a stronger resistance to what we want and feel we need from them.

Conversely, and perhaps counterintuitively, as was the case with Anna in chapter 2, when we have few or no expectations of our parents, there is no pressure on them to "perform," and we are more likely to receive unexpected "gifts" from them.

Consequently, it is best to lower our expectations of our parents and ask ourselves whether they can realistically meet the perceived needs that underlie those expectations. I believe they can't in most cases. Ultimately fulfilling those needs, whether they be the need to be supported, nurtured, or validated, is our responsibility to ourselves.

ACKNOWLEDGE YOUR PARENTS' "GIFTS"

JoAnne's father, who suffered from Parkinson's disease, was a strict disciplinarian. He was often mean and cruel to her and her two older brothers. She says her brothers were bitter and never able to accept her dad for who he was. One brother refused contact all together. JoAnne, however, was able to at least partially forgive her father because she attributed his mean-spirited ways to his suffering with Parkinson's for so many years.

When JoAnne first described her father to me, it was all in negative terms, particularly how he constantly mistreated her brothers. When I asked her whether he had any redeeming qualities, her eyes lit up and a soft smile came to her face as she shared:

"Yes. My father was always so kind and generous and courteous to his friends and acquaintances. He really cared for people a lot. And he was such a dapper dresser. Whenever he walked down the street, he was usually attired in a neat suit and tie, and he always tipped his hat to women in a gentlemanly fashion. My dad was actually quite charming."

I asked whether remembering his positive attributes made acceptance easier. "It definitely did," she said. "It gave me a more balanced perspective of the whole person."

In a similar vein, we should also consider the attributes we received from our parents. In most cases, they are there if you are willing to look for them. Like JoAnne, I had issues about how my father treated me. He was a strict disciplinarian who ruled the roost. It was always his way, and little I did seemed good enough for him. My mother was an emotional, gentle woman who was afraid to stand up to him on my behalf even when I was vastly outmanned. That made me feel unsafe. As a consequence, I was a quiet, reserved child who was reluctant to express his feelings or risk controversy. Not until much later, as a mature adult, did I realize that I had received some important gifts from my parents. My dad was a hardworking, highly principled, and honest businessman, and I feel those traits were passed on to me simply by being around him. In addition, my constantly doing battle with him strengthened my resolve when I later faced difficult challenges—particularly in business. My mother was an artist who enjoyed gardening, and I later found creative expression in oil painting, composing poems, and designing succulent arrangements with palm fronds and other natural foliage.

And, of course, we should not forget the greatest gift our parents have given us: life itself. Although this likely is not in the forefront of the mind of those who have suffered greatly from their parents' transgressions, the gift of life should nonetheless be cherished. I thus believe that, whenever possible, we should make the effort to honor our mother and father, and the gift of acceptance is one way we can do that.

PARENTAL ACCEPTANCE INTENTIONS

Today, with respect to my parents, I will

Be thankful for what they have given me.
Acknowledge their attributes—and limitations.
Remember their personal history.
Lower my expectations of them.
Not blame them for my problems.
Strive to take care of my own needs.
Remember who gave me life.
Honor them!

While some of us find it relatively easy to be compassionate toward, and understanding of, our parents, accepting our siblings and other family members is often more challenging. Let's next take a look at how we can overcome those challenges.

CHAPTER NINE

ACCEPTING OUR SIBLINGS AND FAMILY

"Siblings": Children of the same parents, each of
whom is perfectly normal until they get together.
— *Sam Levenson, American humorist*[1]

RICHARD DUTIFULLY PROMISED HIS father just before
he passed away that he would look after his younger
brother and sister who lived in the South. Almost every
week for a year, he called his siblings to inquire how
they were doing. He also offered his counsel with their
personal struggles. They rarely called him, however,
and when they did it was usually to ask for something—
most often financial assistance. As the months passed,
Richard became more and more resentful because there
was no reciprocation. Still feeling an obligation to his
father, however, he continued calling his siblings but
with similar results.

During a car ride together, I asked Richard whether
he was upset about what happened, and he shared:

"I'm at peace with it now, really. I learned a couple of important things in dealing with my family. One was that I had certain expectations that weren't being met, the main one being that I expected that my brother and sister should at least make some effort to keep in touch with me. When I realized that my anger and resentment were directly related to unmet expectations, I knew I had to let them go. I also didn't like it when my advice was pretty much ignored by them, so I stopped advising."

I told Richard I understood what he was saying, but I wondered how he was able to deal with the fact of having essentially no further communications with his siblings.

His response caught me off guard:

"It dawned on me one day that our family was *never* close. There was never any real connection in our home when we were growing up. We all did our own things and later went our own ways. So why would there be any closeness now? My expectations that there would be were unrealistic. That 'truth' allowed me to accept our family relationship as it was, without any resentment or remorse. That's just the way it was—and is. We now speak infrequently, and I'm okay with that, and I think they are as well. Nothing is forced—and nothing is expected, at least by me. And I totally accept—and am greatly relieved—by that."

"What about the 'promise' to your father," I asked?

"I tried to keep us unified, but for whatever reason, it wasn't important to my siblings. I accept that as well. But here's also what helped: My father himself knew that there never was any closeness among us, as much as he may have wanted it. I suspect he felt partly responsible for it. But he never quite accepted that reality and couldn't let go of his desire that things be different.

That's why he asked me to try—and I did, without success. I now accept that these matters are beyond my power to change."

Understanding Sibling and Family Dynamics

Many siblings have close, supportive bonds with one another. In fact, it's not uncommon to hear sisters or brothers refer to their siblings as their best friends. Regrettably, though, there may be as many siblings that have poor, dysfunctional, and even nonexistent relations with one another. Certain underlying factors often create strong acceptance obstacles, such as age and personality differences, addiction issues, parental favoritism, and variations in parenting methods. Other factors include changes in circumstances, such as when siblings go off to college, get married, have children, or face economic adversity, and when parents get divorced or become ill.

While we have the right to choose our friends and loved ones, with our siblings, we have no choice. They are "involuntary" companions—and usually the longest ones in time. As Dr. Keith Gaynor, senior psychologist with St. John of God Outpatient Psychological Services in Stillorgan, Dublin, aptly puts it, "These two people might never have chosen to be close, if they met in work or in a social situation, but due to an accident of birth they are thrown together every Christmas, wedding and funeral."[2]

I have come to believe that all families are imperfect and to some extent dysfunctional. We easily bring out the worst—and best in one another. We feel freer to scream and yell at one another, and to criticize and scold one another. And at times, to even hate one another.

Given all these permutations and moving parts, is it any wonder that it is often harder to accept our siblings and family members than most others? But that doesn't mean that it isn't better for us—and them—to make an effort to do so. Whether or not blood is thicker than water, it nonetheless is still blood! Maybe it would help if we acknowledge that our families—including ourselves—are imperfect.

To repeat what my father said, "We are stuck together whether we like it or not." So for me, it is important to find ways to get along better within the framework of our particular family dynamic, which is to say, accept our siblings and family as they are. Following are some keys to doing that.

KEYS TO ACCEPTING OUR SIBLINGS AND FAMILY

The following guidelines can help in accepting our siblings and family.

DRAW LINES OF PEACE

Growing up, Larry and his younger sister Beth had a highly divisive relationship. They didn't get along and were constantly butting heads. In their quarrelsome family, Larry was the mediator and Beth the instigator. This dynamic played out well into their adult years, particularly with Larry's two marriages. Both his wives wanted to include Beth in important family events, but she often made things so difficult that, as Larry puts it, "I always was put in the middle, having to choose between my sister and my wives, and of course I chose my wives."

I ran into Larry one day and asked if things had improved between him and his sister, and to my surprise, he said they were getting along much better. When I asked what had changed, he replied:

"I was able to set some boundaries with Beth. It wasn't easy, and it took some time, but we now both abide by them, and in the past year our relationship has improved a lot. While she is still very difficult at times, she is one of the brightest women I know and I really respect her and admire all her accomplishments. I wouldn't say we're real close, but I love her as my sister."

When I probed further as to what kind of boundaries he was referring to, Larry answered:

"I told my sister that I wanted a good relationship with her, but there were certain areas that usually led to more conflict. Our common goal was (and is) to have a working, loving relationship with each other. When one of those topics came up, I just said that the conversation was going someplace that I was uncomfortable with and asked to change the subject. As I said, it took a while, but now she respects those boundaries and we now have some very nice conversations and family get-togethers."

I have always considered reasonable boundaries, compassionately and clearly set, to be "lines of peace"—for both us and others. Like Larry's, they may be in the form of avoiding problematic topics of discussion. They can also be in the form of choosing the type, extent, and frequency of contact you wish to have. For example, you may decide that contact with your sister, brother, or other family member should be one-on-one or by phone, and not at family events or gatherings. The important thing is that whatever boundaries you set should be made kindly and clearly. Not unexpectedly, you may meet resistance and even some resentment, but that need not deter you from setting them. As in Larry's case, it might take some time and effort, but ultimately your choice—and right—to determine what kind of boundaries are appropriate and necessary to avoid unwanted discord are yours to make.

MODERATE YOUR EXPECTATIONS

Just as with accepting our loved ones, children, and parents, moderating our expectations of siblings and other family members is an integral part of accepting them as they are. When we don't, negativity can result, as Sanjay learned.

In responding to an article I wrote on my blog on family expectations, Sanjay explained why he found it important to let go of his unrealistic expectations concerning his family:

"I am facing a problem with loved ones. I developed a very high level of expectations from them, thinking that whatever I suggest or do for them is the best. But many times they did whatever they wanted to, even if they faced pain and hardships. And after a long time now I am able to understand what I was doing wrong and that I should change myself. I have no right to give any suggestions to anyone; I love them intimately and always want them to be happy . . . but it really doesn't matter at all. Everybody has their own life. It's all very complicated. The best thing we can do is to release ourselves from all attachment to any outcome that is based on someone else's actions or inactions! That way we can avoid negativity."

Since our expectations are often the highest with regard to our siblings and family, the consequent resentment and disharmony is often the strongest. Our high expectations in part are likely due to the fact that we feel safer in asserting our desires and needs with our family and because we may look to them to fulfill needs such as support (including financial) and companionship. Whatever the reasons, it behooves us to moderate our expectations as much as we can.

DON'T SPECULATE

Many who speculate about what their families may do or how they may act usually assume the worst. They are mainly governed by FEAR: "*Future Events Already Ruined.*" Negative speculations lead to negative outcomes. Your family will likely sense them, putting themselves on the defensive. Hence, don't plant the seeds of future family disharmony by assuming or anticipating conflict or unpleasant behavior based on past history. For example, if you are apprehensive about sitting at the same table with your wayward brother or sister at a holiday dinner or other important family gathering, don't make any assumptions about how they may act. Instead trust that you will be able to detach from any upsetting behavior or issues that might arise and still enjoy the occasion.

LOOK THROUGH THEIR LENSES

Before judging or reacting strongly to your siblings' or family members' disturbing words and actions, try to view them through their "lens"—one that is likely significantly different from yours. Their conduct is likely based on their perception of past family history and interactions with you, as well as their current life struggles, marital satisfaction, economic situation, emotional state, and such. The more you are able to view your siblings through their lens, the more forgiving and compassionate you can be and the less anger and discomfort you will have. It will also be easier for you to detach from any divisiveness.

BE GRATEFUL FOR WHAT YOUR FAMILY GIVES YOU

Just as in other relationships, instead of dwelling on family members' annoying traits and what you don't like about them, focus on the good that they bring to your life—their support and loyalty, for example. Or the comfort they provide you in times of sickness and need.

DON'T TRY TO CHANGE THEM

Avoid trying to change the actions of your family that annoy you. They are who they are. You can express your displeasure or request that they cease from acting certain ways, but there is little beyond that you can do. And your efforts to do so, particularly if through controlling means like advice giving, criticism, and admonishment, will most likely cause greater divisiveness. You are better served by detaching or changing your role in the relationship.

Examine and Change Your Role in the Relationship

It is easy to overlook our role in a disruptive and disturbing relationship we may have with our family. Maybe you were a bossy big brother or sister who put down your siblings. Maybe you didn't give them the time of day or support activities and involvements that were important to them. It is important that you be introspective—and honest with yourself—as to how your actions or inaction may have exacerbated the family relationship—and still may be doing so.

In my experience, in order to objectively examine my role in a disruptive family situation or occurrence, I had to overcome that ego-based part of me that feels I didn't do anything wrong or that I wasn't at fault. However, when I am objective and truthful enough, I almost always find that I played some role in what transpired. I suspect it will be the same for you.

I have also learned that I always have the choice to change my role in the family dynamic or relationship. I can *choose to* be the person I am today and engage my family from this present-day perspective and maturity, not from the way I was as a child or young adult. As such, I can choose not to expect, not to overreact, and not to pressure. I can also choose to be more tolerant and understanding of my family, as mentioned before. If at times I need some distance and less involvement, I can do that in a thoughtful manner.

As you make these changes and choices, you shorten the space between you and your family polemics, thereby dissolving unnecessary dissension and conflict. A "shift" can occur in which your family feels safer and more trusting of you and reacts and responds to you in a more considerate and loving manner—and therein I believe lies the best hope for bringing the family unity and closeness we may seek or desire.

SIBLING AND FAMILY ACCEPTANCE INTENTIONS

Today, with my siblings and family, I will

Be grateful for what they give me.
Recognize my part in family discord.
Not engage them when they act out.
Consider their struggles and life status.
Be mindful of the person I am today.
Remember that I am not perfect.
Set appropriate boundaries.
Be compassionate toward them.

We have so far looked at accepting those with whom we have love and biological ties and thus likely have a greater incentive and desire to find ways to better accept them. The same is typically not the case with our friends, who come into our lives at different times and settings. To a large extent, we have more of a choice about accepting our friends, whose quirks and idiosyncrasies create their own unique acceptance challenges. Let's take a look at some of them in the next chapter.

CHAPTER TEN

ACCEPTING OUR FRIENDS

> Always be mindful of the kindness and not
> the faults of others.
>
> —*Attributed to The Buddha*

"WE MUST ACCEPT OUR friends as They Are" reads the headline on page 16 of the April 13, 1937, edition of the *Deseret News* in Salt Lake City, followed by the subtitle, "Any Effort to Change Them Inevitably Results in Irritation."[1] It appears in a national advice column by Caroline Chatfield and is addressed to a reader dealing with a tarnished friendship:

"Dear Miss Chatfield:

"At the moment I am in a bad state of mind with my best friend. She is one of those people who always has to be right. No matter how badly she hurts anyone she always has the ready excuse which proves conclusively that she is not in the least to blame. I cannot imagine her saying simply: 'I'm sorry, I was wrong.'

"Her ego constantly seeks recognition from others even at their expense. Still she's rather nice and maybe I shouldn't be so critical. Anyhow, I thought maybe you could smooth me down and help me to have a more pleasant relationship with her. . . ."

Miss Chatfield's response:

"We have to be old and ready to die before we realize that we cannot force our friends to give us what we would have them give us, treat us as we would be treated. And of course it never occurs to us that they can bring complaints against us similar to those we bring against them. We are too intent on adding up what we are getting to realize how little we are giving. The psychologists tell us . . . that the critical get that way because they feel their own failures. Misery loves company. They look around to find flaws in friends and acquaintances and in finding them they take a fiendish delight in pointing those flaws up and out. . . .

"This being the case, shouldn't we pity the friend who isn't big enough or courageous to say, 'I was wrong and I am sorry?' Shouldn't we have sympathy for the little souls who try to pretend they are big and one hundred per cent right about everything? Yes, we should, but this doesn't mean that we enjoy being with them or love and admire them. . . ."

This article makes clear that the struggle of coping with the irritable things our friends say and do is an age-old one. We need to consider the impact—to us and them—of not accepting our friends as they are. A few times in the past I have felt that impact to my regret.

Nonacceptance Creates Resentment

Ethan is a rare individual who didn't have a cell phone or even an answering machine at home. The only way I could reach him was by leaving a message at his office. Consequently, he could reach me whenever he wanted, but I rarely could do the same, particularly in the evenings and on weekends. I felt it was unfair and selfish of him and kept telling him he should get an answering machine. One day he remarked that he could always be reached, and I let him have it. I told him he was inconsiderate and that I resented his being so in control over when we could talk or make plans together. Needless to say, Ethan reacted angrily. I realized how childlike I had acted and apologized the following day, but the damage was done. We didn't speak for two years.

When people don't act or respond the way we expect them to or think they should, we are moved to try to change them—and this is the exact opposite of accepting them. In doing so, we easily become critical, judgmental, and demanding, as I did with Ethan, and that invariably leads to resentment because of the pressure we put on others to be and act other than who they truly are—and who wants to be subjected to such pressure? Certainly, Ethan didn't.

That incident made me realize that we are much better served by releasing our expectations of our friends, accepting them as they are, and instead examining the changes that we can make in our own roles in those relationships. The bottom line for friends and others is *when you expect, you can't accept.*

NONACCEPTANCE UNDERMINES THE BOND

The close bond of a good friendship is deeply rewarding. There is the comforting sense of being connected and knowing that you can trust and rely on one another and that your friends will be there for you in times of need—and you for them—which is particularly valuable in a world in which indifference and distrust are so prevalent. Not accepting our friends for who and how they are severely impacts this bond. They no longer feel safe in confiding in or opening up to us. Feeling that they may be judged or criticized, they instead hold back, resulting in a loss of intimacy.

At times we may feel we are accepting our friends when we really aren't. For example, we may repeatedly encourage them to change certain things that we feel would be good for them. Again, it's that mythical sense of omniscience that resides in us. We may also be judgmental through a disapproving look. Or it may simply be as Miss Chatfield so aptly expressed: "We are too intent on adding up what we are getting to realize how little we are giving."

Before jeopardizing or terminating a friendship—particularly a longstanding one—I encourage you to first try to find ways in which to accept your friends—quirks, limitations and all—while still being true to yourself.

Keys to Accepting Our Friends

Here are some keys that I have found very helpful.

Focus on What You Like and Appreciate about Your Friends

As is the case with our loved ones and family, when we are upset or irritated by our friends, it's easy to lose sight of what we like and enjoy about them. We don't have a balanced perspective of them and their impact on our lives. It's thus important to focus on their qualities: what makes them special and unique to us, their loyalty, having a trusted confidant, the good times that we've shared with them, and so on. We need to remember, too, that no one is perfect, least of all ourselves. Hence, be mindful to see the good in our friends and the good they bring to our life.

Be Tolerant

Tolerance, like humility, leads to acceptance. Tolerance requires us to be open-minded and non-judgmental. It is the recognition that no one is perfect, including ourselves. The following reading from the Al-Anon 12-Step Program's *Courage to Change* daily reader (February 18) explains the close correlation between tolerance and acceptance:

"It is easier to accept the limitations of others when I acknowledge my own. I see now that my thinking has often been distorted, my behavior inconsistent.

If my perceptions of myself have been so inaccurate, how reliable can my perceptions of others be? I really don't know what anyone else should think, feel, or do. Therefore, I can no longer justify intolerance."[2]

In a similar vein, as the often-used refrain goes, what we see in others, including their faults, we likely have in ourselves. If we are not perfect ourselves, what right do we have to expect our friends or others to be? Should we not therefore be more tolerant of them? In that respect, one of the benefits of identifying our own shortcomings, which we will learn to do in chapter 17, is that we will be more tolerant and accepting of others.

BE REALISTIC ABOUT YOUR EXPECTATIONS OF THEM

High expectations of a friend can result in losing a friendship, as it did for me with Ethan. It simply puts too much pressure on them to act and be other than who they truly are. As previously expressed with expectations, we shouldn't look to our friends to fulfill our perceived needs, whether it be for more social engagement, to be acknowledged, or to lift us up when we're feeling down. A good friendship can certainly provide some of these benefits, but ultimately we have to find ways to fulfill those needs ourselves.

RECOGNIZE THAT YOU ARE POWERLESS TO CHANGE THEM

Lea loved hanging out with her friend, Emily. They met in college and roomed together for three years. Lea, who was a planner by nature, particularly enjoyed Emily's easygoing way that frequently led to unscripted fun. However, after they graduated and lived separately, Emily's carefree nature began to wear on her. Lea liked to set times for their get-togethers, whereas Emily liked keeping her schedule loose. Lea explained, "Emily might say something loose like, 'We are going to grab brunch and then go on a hike in the afternoon, if you want to join us.' On other occasions she would change her plans. So I never knew what to expect and that frustrated me a lot, even to the point that I found myself getting resentful."

I saw Lea several months later and asked how things were going between the two of them, and she said much better. I asked what had changed and Lea answered:

"I realized that Emily was not going to change; that's just who she was and I needed to accept that. Her carefree nature was one of the things that I really liked about her. I thus didn't take it so personally anymore. That allowed me to see more clearly what I needed to do to make things better for myself."

"What was that?" I asked.

Lea replied, "I knew it wasn't good for me to rely on Emily for my weekend activities, so I stopped trying to make set plans with her. I realized, too, that I was putting unwanted pressure on her. I also started reaching out to my coworkers and others who also liked to plan more for the weekends. That was a difficult stretch for me at first, but I now have more people to do things with and a greater variety of activities to enjoy. When I get together with Emily now, I accept that things may not start on time or that the planned activity may not actually happen, and that just hanging out with her is enough."

The truth of the matter, as Lea's story demonstrates, is that we are powerless over changing those aspects of friends that annoy or bother us. As with our loved ones and siblings, we can express our wishes and views on how we would like things to be or change in the relationship, but beyond that, it's up to our friends to decide whether they want to make the adjustments. The more we press, the less likely they will change. If they don't or are unable to change, and we wish to maintain the friendship, then it is up to us to examine what changes we are willing to make. For example, Ethan and my relationship resumed several years later but on a different basis and, I believe, a healthier one. I was able to acknowledge that he was very different from most people I knew and released my expectations about when I might talk to him or see him. We saw each other much less frequently but still enjoyed each other's company. Bottom line for me, I am grateful that Ethan has been a true friend at critical points in my life.

WALK IN THEIR SHOES

As with our siblings and family, try to see your friends more through their life history and their present challenges and circumstances. *Life with Great Friends* bloggers Doug and Ann Termining use the phrase "walk in their shoes" to describe the importance of having compassion and understanding for friends. In their words:

"What are we dealing with? What are their limitations? Many limitations come from past hurts. When I know the path of pain that others have walked, I no longer believe they are simply doing this to make my life miserable. Additionally, I gain empathy and understanding for their journey and see them in a new light."[3]

DON'T TAKE THINGS SO PERSONALLY

During Casey's third year at an eastern university she shared a small two-bedroom apartment off campus with three other girls. She spent a lot of time with her roommate, Nina, during the previous summer, rapidly becoming good friends. Casey and Nina both found one of the other girls, Lisa, to be very annoying in some of her ways. Nina was always complaining to Casey about how Lisa "did this and did that."

The next semester Casey became very active in campus affairs and had a part-time job off campus. She also had a boyfriend that she spent time with. As a result, the two didn't hang out as much as in the past. One day Casey shared with me that she was upset at Nina because in spite of all her complaints about Lisa, she had posted photos on Instagram of them hanging out together at a popular college nightspot. Casey told me that she felt Nina was being hypocritical. An interesting conversation between us ensued:

ME: Did you feel slighted by Nina?

CASEY: Yes, for sure.

ME: Do you think your ego was involved, meaning that you were jealous that your good friend went out with Lisa?

CASEY: (smiling): Yeah, I guess I was.

ME: Have you looked at it from Nina's perspective?

CASEY: What do you mean?

ME: Well, that Nina may have been lonely and just wanted to have some fun, and you haven't been as available as you were in the past. That doesn't mean that you're not important to her.

Casey agreed and said she immediately felt better. This little story points out that what a friend may do or say that offends most often has more to do with her and where she is in her life. In other words, it's not about *us*. There likely is no intent to hurt or upset us. Our friend may just be having a bad day or dealing with some personal issues as Nina was. Hence, when the "sting" comes, try to take some time to consider what its real source may be and not take the matter too personally.

ACCEPTANCE DOESN'T MEAN APPROVAL OF THEIR BEHAVIOR

As in other relationships, acceptance of our friends does not mean we approve of their disturbing or displeasing ways. Rather, we are simply seeing them as they are without judgment and then deciding what is best for us within that context. We may, for example, choose not to engage them on certain social and political issues or to reduce the time we spend together. Similarly, we may choose to do only things that we are mutually interested in, such as going to plays, museums, or sporting events. In my case, I have friends I enjoy playing tennis with, friends I enjoy going to art shows and museums with, others I enjoy doing business with, and others I enjoy simply having lunch or dinner with. The point being that I believe we can enjoy the best that our different friends offer us and not look to them for more than that.

Intentions for Accepting Our Friends

Today, with my friends, I will

Focus on what I like and enjoy about them.
Not take things too personally.
Not judge them.
Not pressure them to change.
Not expect too much from them.
Remember they are not perfect.

Accepting our friends as they are is one thing. But what about people who are not our friends? Indeed, what if they're actually our foes and adversaries? Should we make an effort to accept these people as well? Let's next take a look at why it can actually benefit us.

CHAPTER ELEVEN

ACCEPTING OUR FOES

We often give our enemies
the means of our own destruction.

—Aesop "The Eagle and the Arrow"

IN READING THE CHAPTER title, you may be thinking to yourself, "Why in the (bleep) should I accept my
foes? They are the last people I would want to accept!
They only look to cause me harm." I fully understand
those feelings. For years, I felt the same way. It's clearly
unnerving to think about accepting the people that
cause us great grief and even more challenging to do
so. However, when I look back, I now realize that I suffered unnecessarily from my refusal to accept people I
disliked or despised, both in terms of greater personal
anguish and counterproductive responses to their unsa-
vory deeds. This was particularly true in the case of the
business partner in chapter 5 who I felt had betrayed
me. My refusal and inability to even consider accepting
this person for who he was—a manipulative, scheming
businessman with few scruples—resulted in my near
bankruptcy and serious health problems.

With time, I have come to understand the benefits of accepting our foes or adversaries for who they are, whether it be in business, at work, or in social and personal settings—even on the tennis court.

MY UNRELENTING TENNIS FOE

One of my joys is competing in seniors' tennis tournaments, where most players are true competitors and display good sportsmanship in the best sense of the word. But not always. Several years ago I played a first-round match in a tournament against a player who constantly miscalled lines and game scores—both, of course, in his favor. I felt I was a better player than he, but I let his court antics upset me so much, I lost my focus—and the match.

After entering another tournament several months later, I received a call from this person asking me if I would assist him in entering the same tournament. He didn't understand English well and had trouble completing the online entry form. Oh, brother, I thought to myself, do I really want to help him? Yet, something told me that good sportsmanship required me to do so. When the draws for the tournament came out several weeks later, lo and behold, we were matched again in the first round.

I was in the midst of writing this book at the time and I instinctively felt there was a reason this was happening: it gave me the opportunity to accept my opponent for the tennis player that he was—crafty and likely not honest—and not let that impact my game.

In our second match, after I was ahead in the first set, he started with his shenanigans again, frequently misstating scores and sometimes making bad line calls. I tried to remain calm, but internally I was very upset by his antics—so much so that I lost my lead and the match! I left the court so embittered that I vowed never to play him again, even if that meant defaulting the match. I was very discouraged that, despite my efforts, I was still unable to accept this person for who he was.

Unbelievably, two months later, I drew him again in the first round of the largest seniors' tournament in the United States, out of over sixty players in our division! How could that happen? Since I didn't want to put myself through such anguish again, I seriously considered withdrawing from the tournament. Yet I sensed that there had to be some higher meaning to all this and decided to play the match. However, I knew I had to seriously examine what I needed to do to not let my opponent get the best of me yet again.

Here are the strategies I used to finally be able to accept my opponent as he was.

- I told myself that I would not judge or speculate about his motives or character. I would thus not focus on his scheming or cheating. Instead, I considered that there might be other reasons beyond my knowledge—or even his—for his poor court manners. Maybe it was as simple as having poor eyesight! Not passing judgment about him made it easier for me to accept that that's simply the way he was and not spend mental energy worrying about it.

- I practiced gratitude. In this case, I was grateful for having the opportunity to do things differently this time. I was also grateful for being physically fit and being able to play in a beautiful desert environment. This significantly defused my resentment and anxiety about playing him again, and as we entered the court, I harbored no ill feelings toward him.

- I focused on what was within my power to do. I knew I couldn't change my opponent, but I did have the power to focus on watching the ball well and playing my own game, despite whatever he might do during the match. I also requested the presence of a court referee to resolve any line disputes.

  In the match, I fell behind 5–2 in the first set even though he hadn't misbehaved; yet I remained calm and focused, confident in my belief that the outcome was all about me and not him. I then won nine straight games and the match! This was despite my opponent's intentionally slowing down play by taking longer-than-allowed rest periods on side changes and more time between points. None of his diversions angered me or distracted my focus from what I needed to do. Indeed, I played even better.

Of course sports competitors are not the only kinds of foes and adversaries we have to deal with and somehow learn to accept. They come in many forms, including unscrupulous business competitors, overbearing bosses, litigants, unfriendly coworkers, and even bullies.

June, a blog visitor, said that she was constantly being badgered by another employee at work yet received no support from her boss. However, she found constructive ways to take care of herself even in the midst of such an intolerable work environment. June shares,

"In my current situation at my office someone extremely toxic had decided to target me for bullying me, and our boss is too afraid to deal with him. Accepting the situation as it exists helps me to focus my mental energy on coping strategies rather than being upset and wondering why this is happening to me or why I am being targeted."

This is a good example of how acceptance allows us to focus on what we can do to best serve our own interests and thereby reduce the stress and anxiety when dealing with difficult situations. Moreover, our acceptance can lead to unexpected rewards, such as what happened with Dale.

UNEXPECTED BLESSINGS OF ACCEPTING OUR FOES

Dale is a graphic artist at a major studio who enjoys collaborating with his fellow artists on important projects—that is, except with Len, an unfriendly loner who always kept to himself. Dale didn't much care for Len and chose to talk to him only when it was essential to the work. At the same time, however, Dale's nature was such that he didn't like being unfriendly to people.

One year when considering what he would give up during Easter Lent, Dale vowed to make an effort to engage and be friendly toward Len. He thus mustered up the will to wish Len a happy Easter and inquire how he was doing. What followed was totally unexpected.

The two took a coffee break, during which Len revealed that his wife had been battling cancer for several years and how it had taken a toll on their finances and relationship. Dale also learned that they had a common passion in metal sculpture work.

Dale's efforts to accept Len as he was thus resulted in a new friendship. In his words,

"When I decided to engage Len, I never could have imagined that we would connect like we did and have so many mutual interests. Len was really going through a lot of adversity in his personal life and it clearly accounted for the way he was at work with everyone. We found common grounds and our working relationship improved significantly. Several years later he retired and moved to the Midwest, but we still talk to one another about our latest sculpting projects."

Several years ago I had a tenant whose business had rapidly grown and outgrew its warehouse space at one of my properties. It created serious problems because his delivery trucks constantly unloaded bulky inventory in parking areas at the property, impeding the adjacent tenant's access to his own warehouse and parking spaces. Since the tenant had doubled the size of his staff, parking was reduced for other tenants as well. These acts were in clear violation of the terms of the tenant's lease.

The tenant in the adjoining unit complained to us that his business was suffering and showed us photos documenting the obstructions. We talked to the problem tenant and showed him the photos. He denied that the unloading of inventory obstructed access for his neighbor yet complied for a few days, but then he went back to unloading where he was not supposed to. The adjacent tenant moved out of his space a month later.

At this point, I felt we had two options. We could sue for monetary damages for breach of the lease agreement and loss of the other tenant and also seek an injunction against further lease violations. Or we could pay for costly parking monitors to help reduce the infractions. Because of my anger about what had happened and the tenant's denial of any wrongdoing, my first reaction was to have our attorney file suit.

When I took the weekend to think further about the situation, another option began to evolve. I realized that the underlying truths were

1. The tenant was doing what he was doing because he had no real choice given his rapid growth, not because he was intentionally trying to harm anyone. As they often say in mob films, "It's nothing personal." I accepted that it wasn't. That defused my anger.

2. It would take money, time and a lot of aggravation to pursue legal action, and even though we would likely prevail, we might not be able to collect on the judgment, and further, the tenant's lease would expire by the time we got to court.

I concluded that I needed to accept the tenant and situation for what it was. The tenant was acting out of "business survival" and I had little chance of stopping him. So I chose a third option: *do nothing* and see how things played out. I also served notice that the tenant's rent would be increased significantly if he remained after his lease expired. The tenant moved out two months later.

The silver lining to the story is that a new tenant immediately leased the space at a 20 percent higher rate, increasing both our operating profit and the value of the property. Still, accepting our foes and adversaries as they are is never easy.

KEYS TO ACCEPTING OUR FOES

Particularly in dealing with our foes, it is important to remember what acceptance *doesn't* mean. We are not excusing or condoning what our foe did or does. Nor does it mean that we have to negate our values and principles or not be able to take care of ourselves. Rather it is only by accepting our adversaries as they are that we will be able to recognize the choices and options that serve us best, as I did in my final tennis match and as June did with her toxic coworker. Why? As I repeatedly emphasize, with acceptance, the focus changes from others to *you*—and what you can do to better serve your own needs.

DON'T ACT OR REACT IMPULSIVELY

Pause and take the time to assess what's really at stake with your grievance against someone and its overall importance. In doing so, consider whether you can realistically expect to change the person or what he is doing, as I did with my problem tenant. Remember that even if you feel you can have some impact on your adversary, consider whether any success is worth the cost and energy—and anguish. You can gain more "pause time" by asking yourself such questions as these: *"Is this something that is best left alone for now?"* and *"Am I making a mountain of a molehill?"*

Address Your Fears

Similarly, our fears of what an adversary—such as a business competitor—can or will do to harm us, make us reactive instead of realistically addressing what we can do to protect or take care of ourselves. It's easy to speculate in a negative manner or fall into the "False Evidence Appearing Real" fear mode. When fear so dominates our thoughts and actions, there is little hope of accepting our adversary in a manner that allows us to make the choices that best serve us—whether it's in work or business, on the playing field, or in our social affairs.

Most fears are illusory; they diminish and even leave once they are examined closely. As mentioned before, we need to first identify them as specifically as we can and then address them.

Worst-case scenario exercises are very helpful in providing us with needed objectivity and a balanced perspective of the situation. For example, in my tennis story (and I believe this to be true in most sports and other competitions), my worst fear was losing to a devious opponent in a big tournament. Yet I have lost a lot of times in big tournaments, so what's really the big deal about another loss? Nothing. It's not going to make me a worse player—and certainly not a worse person!

Look through Their Lenses

It can soften the sharp edge of your resentment if you try to see things from their perspective. Many—perhaps even most—times, people's behavior is based on their fears, anxieties, insecurities, and self-interests and not on any intent to harm us. As I did with my problem tenant, when we view the actions of perceived foes and adversaries through their lenses, it is easier to detach ourselves from their conduct and make decisions or responses that are in our best interest.

PROCESS YOUR ANGER

Remy was shocked when her husband Tim's former wife, Susan, served papers on him demanding a doubling of child-support payments. Susan's new husband earned a lot more than they did and lived in a large home in an affluent neighborhood of Studio City, California. What made it all the more upsetting was that Remy and Susan had become good friends and the couples frequently socialized. As Remy described the relationship, "All of us had an almost idyllic relationship."

To make matters even worse, Remy and Tim had just purchased a larger home in anticipation of having a child of their own. Now her dream of having her own child went by the wayside because she would have to work full time to help make the increased child support and house payments. Remy felt betrayed by Susan and stopped talking to her. She says,

"This incident elicited the most anger and desperation I've ever felt in my lifetime at the time. I felt robbed by this woman—taking my husband's money that was also *my* money. It was painful to see her driving around in the new expensive SUV she bought—using what I considered my money. The daily rage I felt ate away at me. I tried antidepressants, talk therapy, joined a father's rights group—but nothing worked."

Spring forward four years. Remy and Susan were friends again. When I asked Remy how she came to accept someone who had made her life so difficult, she replied:

"I realized I was tired of being angry and resentful. It takes too much energy and there was nothing I could do about the situation that plagued me. I learned that I *do* have the ability to not only fully recover from anger and desperation but also to reengage the person who made me angry—and this led to an even stronger relationship. On so many levels, I really liked Susan, and I was mourning the loss of this friend, whether or not I realized it.

"When our finances improved, I became pregnant with my own son and the two of us shared pregnancy stories. And when I went into labor, she was a wonderful help. Since this incident, I have moved forward with the confidence that I can handle almost anything."

It's only natural—only human if you will—to be upset or resentful when someone acts badly toward us. What is important, however, is that these feelings be addressed and processed in a timely manner and not be allowed to linger. Continuing to harbor anger and resentment hurts mainly ourselves. As the late Carrie Fisher says in her book *Wishful Drinking*, "Resentment is like drinking a poison and waiting for the other person to die."[1] I would add to that, "Or until we are too sick to take it anymore!" Anger obscures what is objectively at stake, as well as what we can do to remedy it.

Whatever has happened or been done to us by another, we still have a choice in the matter. We can remain enmeshed in our anger and resentment, or we can try to find ways to defuse it before we become "too sick." It need not be viewed as a matter of right or wrong. Even if we are in the right, it is to little avail if we remain bogged down by these negative feelings. And yes, retaliation is also an option, but at best, it makes us feel better for only a short while (if that) and far more likely serves mainly to exacerbate our torment.

CONSIDER YOUR ROLE IN THE GRIEVANCE

You should always consider whether you had some role in the upsetting behavior of others. For example, were you smug, rude, or dismissive toward them? Did you misconstrue what they said or did? It takes courage and self-honesty to admit you may be at least partly at fault as well. I believe you should always examine whether you were responsible in some way.

Sometimes we can't see our part in what transpired because the "sting" makes that difficult. With few exceptions, I have learned that no matter how innocent or right I thought I was about something that upset me, I was in some way responsible. You may need to overcome the feeling you were wronged before you can begin to acknowledge your part in the matter. One thing is clear, though. The sooner we ask the question and examine what our role may have been, the sooner our resentment leaves.

LOOK FOR THE GOOD IN WHAT HAPPENED

When we feel harmed by the actions of others, it's easy to become mired in our hurt and pain. We feel abused, let down, even betrayed, as I did with my former business partner. Certainly, we feel nothing positive at the time. However, just as with the inquiries above, it takes time and reflection to become aware that there may also be some good things that were generated by the adversity.

In the case with my business partner, several unexpected but very valuable things emerged from it. First, he was a very astute businessman and I learned a lot from him during the years we worked together, which I later applied in my own business dealings with great success. Second, I learned how well I could take care of myself under adverse circumstances, something about which I always had doubts. I gave this very powerful person the fight of his life. I managed to draw on my inner resources and talents to resist him every step along the way. I never knew I could be so resourceful. And third, it changed the direction and trajectory of my career. I went from being exclusively beholden to one individual to enjoying the freedom, independence, and empowerment of being the head of a real estate investment company that acquired and managed investments for myself and a diversified group of investor/partners.

I deeply believe that these were blessings I could not have received in any other manner. They certainly were not anticipated at the time I felt betrayed, but they definitely were triggered through overcoming my anger and finally accepting this person for who he was. This dynamic is neither a unique nor an uncommon occurrence. We repeatedly hear of it by such expressions as "the good that comes from the bad" and the "yin and yang" of life. It may come in the form of new friendships, such as with Dale and Len; financial gains, such as with my problem tenant; and almost always, in making better choices for ourselves.

AN ACCEPTANCE CHALLENGE

The next time you deal with an adversary, an unpleasant person—or even a perceived "enemy" for that matter—I challenge you to try accepting her as she is. In doing so, don't overreact or retaliate. Depersonalize the situation the best you can. Pause to process your anger and fear. Consider whether you had any part in what occurred. Don't assume that there was an intention to harm you. In doing these things, note whether you feel calmer, more grounded, less annoyed, more focused on taking care of your needs, and more able to make better decisions.

There is one type of perennial foe that seems to be everywhere we go, always in our face, and forever causing us grief and anxiety. It's a challenge to survive these foes, let alone accept them. But there are some ways, as we will see in the next chapter.

CHAPTER TWELVE

ACCEPTING—AND SURVIVING—CONTROL FREAKS

When we don't accept control freaks, we give them considerably more power over our lives than they otherwise have.

—*Daniel Miller,* Losing Control, Finding Serenity

JUST AS WITH ACCEPTING foes, in seeing this chapter's title, you may be thinking, "Why should I accept control freaks? I can't stand them!" "They only make my life miserable." You clearly are not alone in thinking such things. Donna, a visitor to my blog, describes the emotional pain of living with a control freak:

"Living with a control freak is extremely hard as they first trap you in their web, make you believe that they are the only ones that can love you like they do, they appear at first to do everything for you . . . they shower you with everything. It's merely a honey trap for later on! . . . Don't feel sorry for them as they know what they are doing!"

What is a control freak? The *Merriam-Webster Dictionary* defines *control freak* as "a person whose behavior indicates a powerful need to control people or circumstances in everyday matters." The *Cambridge Dictionary* defines the term as "someone who is determined to make things happen exactly the way they want and who tries to make other people do what they want."

For most people, I think, it's more a matter of "you know one when you see or experience one," or as in Donna's case above, when you live with one. In terms of practicing acceptance in this chapter, I include excessive controllers such as micromanagers, nitpickers, and perfectionists.

In any event, there is a good reason for accepting control freaks and excessive controllers: *we must accept them in order to free ourselves from them.* A paradox? Perhaps. Certainly counterintuitive. But the truth of the matter is, it is the best way to minimize their grip on us. To be sure, this is no easy task—they so easily can get under our skin! It helps to understand them better.

UNDERSTANDING CONTROL FREAK DYNAMICS

Pure and simple, controllers are fear driven. Almost everything they do—or not do—is because of some underlying fear or anxiety often unbeknownst to them. They are particularly afraid of uncertainty, the unknown, and of what the future holds. Consequently, they are obsessed and worried about "what ifs," "what I should dos," and "what could happens" rather than accepting and trusting "what is." As a result, they don't allow events to take their natural course or people to do their own thing. At their core, controllers fear their very survival—and their death. In a very real way, *controllers don't trust life!*

As such, control freaks live a life filled with grand illusions about the efficacy of control. They believe control works and that they need it to "survive." Indeed, they are insecure without control. How do I know these things? As I explained in the introduction, I was a controller extraordinaire! I constantly tried to control everything and everyone—particularly those closest to me. Everything had to pass my close scrutiny and be done my way. That's what I wrongly felt was necessary to satisfy my needs and achieve what I wanted in life.

Given these "credentials," allow me to share my knowledge and experience about what makes control freaks tick and what you can do to survive them. It requires an understanding of these grand illusions, or more accurately, grand myths.

FIVE GRAND MYTHS OF CONTROL FREAKS

Myth #1: *Control freaks believe they have the power to significantly change others.*

Truth: The short of it is that control freaks are not nearly as powerful as they believe. As stated before, the only ones who can meaningfully change people's ways are the people themselves—and then only if they so choose and are able to do so. Simply put, control freaks are effectively powerless over changing others in any real sense. If allowed, they can make others feel a lot of things—shameful, rattled, and overwhelmed, for example—but they can't make them *better*.

Myth #2: *Control freaks believe control will make them happier.*

Truth: Just the opposite. Constantly trying to control others and things is a prescription for greater worry and anxiety and overall "dis-ease." How can it be otherwise, given the unrelenting obsessiveness that underlies their controlling actions?

Myth #3: *Control freaks believe that controlling others and things gives them more control over their own lives.*

Truth: Again, just the opposite. The only way they can gain more control over their life—to the extent that one really can—is through letting go of control. Which is to say, you only *gain* control by *losing* control. Consequently, by trying so hard to control others and things, their own lives spin more out of control. Sadly, but certainly not unexpectedly, it becomes a vicious cycle for them; as their lives spin deeper out of control, they resort to even more control to stop the accelerating spiral, only to feed it more.

Myth #4: *Control freaks consider themselves to be confident, secure, and fearless.*

Truth: Not true. If control freaks were truly confident, secure, and fearless, they would be willing to allow life's natural currents to flow freely and without their intervention, with faith and trust that they could safely navigate them. How many controllers do you know that take things in stride or go with the flow? Not many—maybe none, I suspect.

Myth #5: *Control freaks believe they know what's best for others.*

Truth: Almost laughable. Control freaks seldom know what's best for themselves, let alone others. Focusing so much on trying to change or control others leaves little room for honest introspection. Yet, they assume—erroneously and often arrogantly—that what works for them will also work for others. I doubt that any control freak has ever been accused of being too humble!

KEYS TO ACCEPTING AND SURVIVING CONTROL FREAKS

With a better understanding of how control freaks think and what they believe, we can formulate some effective tools and strategies for dealing with them.

DON'T TAKE THEIR EXHORTATIONS AND ACTIONS PERSONALLY

When control freaks start ranting, pressuring, and criticizing, do your best not to take any of it personally. Remember that it's not about you. It's all about them, meaning their fears and apprehensions and insecurities. Thus, the more you can detach yourself from their behavior, the less impact they will have on your well-being.

Remain Calm and Don't Engage Them

It's almost always best not to engage control freaks. Control freaks are "crazy makers," and confronting them usually only feeds their "frenzy." Reasoning with them also doesn't work because their fears overcome any sense of reason. It is best for you—and them for that matter—to remain calm as they vent. Doing so can subliminally defuse their fears. Consequently, most of the time it is best to just listen and not say too much— unless of course, your welfare and safety are involved. If you do feel the need to firmly stand your ground, try to do so in a calm, unemotional manner.

Act Confidently around Them

Back in the day when I was a major controller, the one thing that relieved my anxiety was dealing with competent, confident people—particularly at work. It was relatively easy for me to relinquish control in such cases. Why? Because I trusted that these people were as good as I at what they did—maybe even better—and that alleviated my fear and anxiety.

Consequently, act as confidently and self-assuredly as you can around controllers. You will be surprised at how much your self-confidence will comfort them. To them, at least someone has their house in order! Even if you aren't truly confident, do your best to act as if you are. The expression "fake it until you make it" is apropos here.

Reassure Them

Control freaks need constant reassurance. It alleviates their fears and anxieties. Remember, their lives are filled with constant "what might happens." Most worry about whether important matters will be done right and on time—and about what dreadful consequences will ensue if they aren't. It is thus no surprise that control freaks sleep poorly, find it difficult to have fun, and have deeper frown lines than laugh lines.

Thus, reassure the controllers in your life that everything will be okay, that things will work out for them. They need to hear (usually more than once) and feel that. It eases the "dangers" and "nightmares"—mostly fictional—that they repeatedly script for themselves. Here are some examples of what you might say:

To a loved one: "Dear, don't worry, everything will be okay," or "Sweetheart, is there anything I can do to help?"

To your boss: "Don't worry, I'll make sure things are handled properly," or "No problem. I'm on it."

Get the idea? You should of course use words and reassurances that feel right to you under the circumstances and with respect to the controllers and their concerns.

Show Them Some Compassion

Yes, you are reading this correctly. If you are thinking, Why should I be compassionate toward control freaks when they make my life so miserable? again you are not alone. Several years ago I received a lot of flack after I posted on my blog a short article titled "Control

Freaks Suffer, Too—and You Can Help Them!" The idea of helping control freaks was repulsive to some blog visitors, as indicated by the following visitor response:

"Control freaks find themselves God on this earth. You have to be controlled like a puppet. Only then will you know what a miserable trap you are in. I for one will never feel sorry for them because they have cheated us and continue to cheat with utmost greed."

I understand that you may have similar feelings, so let me explain why I believe that having some compassion toward control freaks helps in accepting—and surviving—them. As I explained in chapter 3, true acceptance requires that we accept others *without* harboring negative feelings, particularly anger and resentment. If we harbor such feelings, it is unlikely that we can free ourselves from their rigid clasp. It can defuse your anger and resentment if you consider that control freaks likely have an anxiety disorder that deprives them of serenity and connection with their loved ones and what friends they have. With lives so out of balance, we can feel some compassion for them. That doesn't mean we have to like them or condone what they do; rather, just try to understand what's behind their actions.

That being said, however, I want to be very clear that you should never tolerate violence or physical or extreme emotional abuse from a control freak. If you feel you are in harm's way, do not hesitate to seek the help of others or, when you feel it is necessary, the police.

I encourage you to try using these strategies as a means of accepting control freaks for who and what they are. If you are even partially successful, it will lessen their hold over you and that's no small blessing!

CONTROL FREAKS ACCEPTANCE INTENTIONS

Today, with respect to the controllers in my life, I will

Not take what they do personally.
Recognize the fears and anxieties that drive them.
Remain calm and not engage them.
Not be a doormat.
Act confidently around them.
Reassure them that everything will be okay.

Now that we've considered some effective tools and strategies to help us accept others as they are, let's look at how we can learn to accept things or circumstances and situations as they are or, as some would say, "accept life on life's terms."

PART III

ACCEPTING CHANGE
AND ADVERSITY

CHAPTER THIRTEEN

ACCEPTING LIMITATIONS AND INFIRMITIES

Once we accept our limits,
we go beyond them.

—Albert Einstein

DR. GEORGE PATTERSON EXUDED unbridled joy and enthusiasm whenever I saw him. "Dr. George," as he was fondly called by his friends and clients, was one of those larger-than-life personalities to which people were instinctively drawn. I had the good fortune to meet him several years ago. We agreed to get together at his favorite restaurant with the goal of discussing a keynote address I would be giving at an addiction recovery center in Pasadena that he headed. As I entered the restaurant, Dr. George greeted me with a warm, wide smile and bright eyes. As soon as we sat down at the table, he asked me whether I had ever been fly-fishing. I learned that fly-fishing was his life passion and that he and his good friend, Dr. Joseph Bailey, for the past fifteen years had conducted "Fly Fishing for the Mind" seminars at fly-fishing hot spots around the world.

Enthralled by Dr. George's sense of excitement and joy, I signed myself and my son Brandon up for his upcoming seminar in the Sian Ka'an Biosphere Reserve at the far end of Mexico's Yucatan Peninsula. We learned how the challenges of fly-fishing were closely linked to life's emotional challenges, including anger, impatience, disappointment, undue expectations, and such.

As my friendship with Dr. George quickly grew, I learned that he had survived pancreatic cancer and was living for years with constant breathing difficulties due to having only one lung. At the time we met, he was also undergoing treatment for recurring colon cancer. Yet, despite all these health limitations, Dr. George brightened every room he entered and was an inspiration and mentor to many people, myself included, freely offering his profound life insights and wisdom to others.

There is no question in my mind why Dr. George had so much joy in his life, despite all his hardships. He lived in acceptance every day. He accepted his life as it was, limitations and all, and that allowed him to enjoy the things he still was able to do, including teaching others the techniques of fly-fishing in his backyard swimming pool, playing the piano at sing-alongs, and teaching at seminaries and addiction rehab centers. He even managed to hit tennis balls with me for short periods of time with a portable oxygen tank harnessed to his back.

Most of us don't have to face serious health and physical limitations until we're older. Others, however, like Moe Mernick, must face the formidable challenge of accepting their limitations from a very early age if they wish to enjoy a brighter future.

Moe began stuttering when he was three years old. It was daunting for him to speak up in class or meet new friends. He was often laughed at when he couldn't say his name or "hello." He was miserable and constantly wondered what life would have in store for him. Would he ever pass a job interview? Would a girl want to marry him? And painfully, what would it sound like when he read bedtime stories to his kids?

Today, however, having received his master of business administration degree from Tel Aviv University, Moe now lectures at Jewish education programs in the United States, Canada, Europe, and Australia. He also mentors entrepreneurs where he works at a high-tech startup in Tel Aviv. And, contrary to his apprehensions, he now is happily married with children.

What happened? Moe says, "The ultimate turning point happened when I began to *accept* my stutter. No longer did I have to hide from it—it was simply a part of who I was. We all have our challenges—stuttering was mine. It was finally time to live. Thus began my journey to find my inner voice."[1]

Moe's story (like Greg's in chapter 1 and Karl's and Chris's in chapter 2) is an inspiring example of how accepting our limitations can be a catalyst for personal growth and new opportunities. That's because acceptance triggers a critical *shift* in focus from what we can't change or control to what we can. On the other hand, when you don't accept your limitations, you risk exacerbating them. I can painfully attest to this firsthand.

CONSEQUENCES OF NONACCEPTANCE

Not long ago, I reached the finals in a seniors' division of the 65th Annual Santa Monica Tennis Tournament. I was playing the best tennis of my life and quickly jumped to a commanding lead in the first set. Then, while dropping back for a high lob, I felt a twinge in the upper inside of my left leg. Hoping the injury was not serious, I continued playing the game but lost. Still leading in the set, I couldn't reach certain balls in the next game and lost that one too. By that time it was obvious to my opponent that my mobility was severely restricted. My painful squeals made that clear! He then began hitting drop shots, followed by shots to the wide left and right. I couldn't reach the balls and he easily closed out the first set.

My injury had worsened. But did I accept my limitations and concede the match? Of course not. I wanted too badly to win an important tournament. (Not exactly a healthy ego!) I kept telling (fooling, really) myself that there must be some way to win. I tried blasting my shots deep across the net, trying to quickly win points without having to run. That worked for one game, but my opponent adjusted his tactics and ended up winning the second set (and the match) 6–1.

But that was the least of my discomfort. By continuing to play, I severely strained my abductor muscles in the groin area. Instead of not being able to play for a week or so, I ended up not being able to play for five months and missed several major tournaments.

Still, my setback was minor when compared to the

serious consequences of not accepting more serious health issues. A prime example is Therese Borchard, who constantly struggles with accepting the severe constraints caused by her chronic depression. A successful writer and high achiever for years, she continually gets caught in the vicious cycle between taking on too much and then becoming so depleted that she can barely function at all. In battling the limitations of her mood disorder, she is very much aware of the consequences of not accepting her infirmity. Therese says:

"A very clear pattern has emerged over the last ten years. Too much stress in my life triggers a severe breakdown. So I have to make the 'phone calls of shame,' where I explain to editors and other executives that I am too ill to make the deadlines I had committed to or that I can't handle the project at this time. . . . My cognitive functions are somewhere in the public sewer system."

When her stress leaves and she feels better, she starts adding responsibilities little by little. A writing job here and there, until she's at over forty hours a week again. Stress and fits of frustration return. After a week of crying, sleepless nights, and fights with her husband, Therese says the truth hits her in the gut: "I'm not normal and can't keep a normal schedule."

Today, Therese willingly turns down prestigious writing assignments because, she says, "I would very much like not to have to wear a paper robe and eat rubber chicken in a room where a bunch of other paper robes fight over the remote control. . . . I guess I don't believe everything is possible anymore. Not for people with chronic depression. I believe wisdom comes with knowing your limitations and living within them."[2]

ACCEPTANCE IMPROVES
QUALITY OF LIFE

Gabrielle's quality of life improved when she finally accepted that her severe bipolar disorder controlled her and not the other way around. Deep depression is the mainstay of the condition. It makes her feel weak, helpless, and hopeless. Gabrielle says, "The condition is like going through a long dark stench and vermin-ridden sewer pipe."

A determined fighter by nature, her instincts were to fight hard in trying to manage her condition rather than let it control her. But it was to no avail. She finally came to accept that her condition really managed her and that it was best to not fight it. She says at first it felt like defeat, but now she acknowledges the benefits:

"It certainly beats repeatedly banging my head against the bipolar wall. It also conserves energy that is then at my disposal for me to enjoy during the days of fresh air and sunshine."[3]

Sarah Hackley suffers from chronic migraines. She describes her disease as going in circles—the attacks moving from intractable to episodic to dormant and then back again. When she's migraine free, she says she has so much energy that she feels invincible and is boundlessly optimistic and eternally chipper. This all goes, however, when her migraines return. She's then fatigued and exhausted and needs at least five hours more sleep each night. What's even worse for her is that she becomes very irritable and loses her positivity.

Through acceptance, however, Sarah found a better way to handle the constant transitions:

"Thankfully there are ways to ease these transitions. Accepting my limitations seems to be the biggest. When we're deep into a cycle of frequent intense migraine, we experience mood changes and oscillations in our energy levels . . . we all find ourselves unable to maintain the levels of productivity and positivity that we maintained prior to the chronic attacks. Accepting this, accepting that we are going to feel 'less than' our usual selves for a period of time helps.

"For me, it reminds me that this is only my current state of being. That eventually, the attacks will ebb—even if it takes years—and I will gradually begin to feel more like myself. It also helps me separate my 'self,' my core identity, from the set of feelings and behaviors that chronic migraine triggers. It enables me to see that I am not those feelings, and that is crucial, I feel, to warding off depression and maintaining a positive image."[4]

Recent medical research confirms that accepting our limitations improves our quality of life. In a study of one hundred heart patients in Poland, researchers found that those patients who adapted to their illness reported much more energy, less pain, a brighter outlook, and better sleep than those who couldn't accept theirs. When the researchers compared patients' acceptance levels with their symptoms and quality-of-life responses, they found that the people who scored higher in acceptance of their illness had a much better quality of life.

Very importantly, the study found that acceptance was the *only* independent predictor of quality of life.[5]

KEYS TO ACCEPTING OUR LIMITATIONS

Accepting health and lifestyle limitations and conditions is a formidable challenge for most people. As these stories demonstrate, success depends on maintaining certain positive mind-sets and attitudes, acknowledging the underlying reality, and being able to separate the "impairment" from the person. There are additional keys to accepting our limitations. It starts with letting go of denial.

LET GO OF DENIAL

As mentioned in chapter 4, denial is initially helpful in countering the debilitating shock of unexpected adversity because it gives people time to begin to process traumatic changes in their lives. However, prolonged denial impedes learning constructive ways to alleviate our adversity. It also risks worsening the adversity, like it did with my tennis.

Part of denial is the tendency to resist accepting the diagnosis of one's limitation or infirmity. After all, who wants to think that she can no longer do things that are important to her? Lana Barhum, who suffers from rheumatoid arthritis and fibromyalgia syndrome, stresses the importance of accepting the original diagnosis:

"Once you are diagnosed with any disease, invisible condition, and/or chronic illness, it will always be a part of your life and the sooner that you accept your diagnosis, the sooner you can learn how to live with your disease. It is also how you will cope and how you will learn to understand that your diagnosis isn't a death sentence. The only thing that your diagnosis has to be is something you have to live with. Once you accept it, you can learn how exactly you will do that. . . . The disease might be your new reality but learning to be flexible means that you accept chronic illness in your life, not that you give up."[6]

Thus, letting go of denial provides a healthier perception of your situation and what you can realistically do about it.

RECOGNIZE WHAT YOU CAN NO LONGER CONTROL—AND WHAT YOU CAN

Like Therese and Gabrielle, many people try to control their condition, whereas the hard truth is that their condition controls them. Until you are able to stop trying to change what you are powerless over, you will not be able to clearly see the constructive steps you can take to adapt to it.

Lana Barhum's life, for example, didn't begin to change until she adapted to her disease rather than trying to fight it. She says, "I learned to accept that I had no control of what happened but I had control of the response I had when other obstacles impeded my life. . . . what the illness doesn't control is how we respond, how we fight back and how we go on the defense against the war waging inside our bodies."

Lana educated herself about her illness and sought support from others who were living with the disease. She learned to pace herself, surrounded herself with emotional support, and became a support-group advocate for people suffering with the same infirmities. These were all important actions that were within her power to accomplish.

It is thus important to be clear about what you can control or change and what you can't, what you are powerless over and what you're not. In almost all cases, trying to control your limitation or infirmity will only make matters worse. Conversely, when you accept your powerlessness over the changes caused by your limitations, you are better able to recognize what you can do to ameliorate them, as these stories illustrate.

MAINTAIN REALISTIC EXPECTATIONS

In dealing with our limitations, at some point we realize—albeit perhaps begrudgingly—that we must moderate our expectations of what we are able to do. We can no longer do the things we previously could or at least in the same manner. Our "present" has changed, and like it or not, we need to reduce our expectations to comport with it. With my tennis, for example, I kept injuring my back because of the physical toll of playing singles—chasing too many balls and serving more frequently. It took repeated back injuries that rendered me unable to play for months at a time before I finally accepted that my tennis expectations at my age were unrealistic. I switched to playing doubles and was still able to enjoy my favorite sport.

Most expectations are based on a belief that life is more or less predictable and certain. But life is really not that way. It is in constant flux and innately impermanent. Indeed, much of the difficulty we have in accepting our limitations and infirmities derives from not embracing life's impermanence.

EMBRACE LIFE'S IMPERMANENCE

Our reliance on life and things being fixed or permanent impacts our ability to handle the unexpected when it comes—as it inevitably will. The Buddhist monk Thich Nhat Hanh describes the suffering caused by resistance to impermanence very simply:

"It's not impermanence that makes us suffer. What makes us suffer is wanting things to be permanent when they are not."[7]

Does it really help that much, though, to accept life's impermanence? Brad Zebrack learned that it did after he had cancer.

Brad was diagnosed with Hodgkin's lymphoma in 1985 at age twenty-five. Rendered sterile by the harsh chemotherapy he was given, he faced a life without children, and his desire to be a middle school teacher was put on hold. After twelve months of intense treatment, he beat his cancer. Motivated by his desire to increase awareness for cancer survivorship, he and his girlfriend, Joanne (now his wife), embarked on an eleven-thousand-mile bike ride around the United States to raise money for the National Coalition for Cancer Survivorship, stopping at cancer centers to visit cancer patients.

Afterward he moved to Michigan where he earned a doctorate in social work and medical sociology and thereafter became an oncology social worker, studying the impact of cancer on adolescents and young adults. Now a professor at the University of Michigan School of Social Work, Brad continues to help young cancer survivors by teaching the importance of life's impermanence as a means of accepting their condition. He poetically describes it as follows:

"Mountains in the distance. Solid and imposing. Immovable. Wake up tomorrow and they are still there. But look closer. Wind blows dust. Rocks and boulders tumble. Rains erode. The mountain is alive and changing. Impermanence. We wake each morning and count on the permanence of our surroundings. Our spouse or partner. Our parents. Our children. Water from the spigot. A morning cup of coffee or afternoon tea. The routines that get us through the day. This is called 'taking life for granted.' Yet impermanence surrounds us.

"Cancer awakens our ability to experience impermanence, including our own mortality. It reminds us that our lives—all lives—will ultimately end, that mortality is the only certainty. So what can we really control? 'Letting Go' awakens us to the realities of impermanence . . . ."[8]

In essence, the suffering from our limitations and infirmities lies in the space between what we want or expect and what really exists. The more we are able to embrace "what is," the more we narrow that space and the suffering within it. In that sense, practicing acceptance and embracing impermanence are the same thing.

GRIEVE YOUR LOSS

It's important to grieve our losses. No longer being able to play our favorite sport, drive a car, hold a baby, sew, cook, or do the things we once were able to do are very real and painful losses. Acceptance comes sooner with grieving or mourning our losses. Ted Wiard, founder of Golden Willow Retreat healing center in Taos, New Mexico, and a certified therapist and grief counselor, says that grief is a lifetime process that helps us heal from a loss. He states that the process can be difficult because we have to redefine ourselves and accept that in loss we metaphorically die as well and move into a new phase of our life. However, once we are able to accept that, we can bring our past wisdom and experiences into our present life.

In Ted's words, "The idea is to honor your past while not being confined, defined and captured by your past . . . . Celebrating change as progress and growth will give you the opportunity to experience the magnificence of the day and celebrate life."[9]

PRACTICE GRATITUDE

Being mindful of the things we are still able to do and the positive things that remain in our lives provides a much-needed counterbalance when we are mired in the loneliness and despair that accompany severe limitations and illnesses. Being grateful for the love and support of family and close friends and having access to good doctors and support groups, for example, can alleviate suffering. So can being grateful for the wisdom we gain with each passing year and the opportunity to share it with others.

I don't suggest practicing gratitude lightly. I fully realize how much easier it is to say than do when one is overcome with despair associated with major setbacks. It may take considerable time and grieving before one can think about being grateful. But it is true that gratitude helps replace despair and resentment. Hence, when you are able, consider practicing gratitude on a daily basis upon waking, during the day, or before going to sleep at night. One way is to make a daily gratitude list.

Another is to share what you are grateful for with others. Still another is to do a daily gratitude meditation, in which you think about the things you are grateful for as you slowly inhale in and breathe out.

LIMITATIONS AND INFIRMITIES INTENTIONS

Today, with respect to my limitations and infirmities, I will

Not be in denial of them.
Be realistic about what I can do.
Be grateful for the good things still in my life.
Be aware of what I cannot control.
Grieve my losses.
Remember that they do not define who I am.

There is one set of limitations we all have to accept at some point in our lives: the losses that come with aging. Let's see how we can make that phase of our lives easier and even rewarding.

CHAPTER FOURTEEN

ACCEPTING THE LOSSES
OF AGING

"The best part of the art of living is to know how to
grow old gracefully."
—*Eric Hoffer, American Philosopher (1898–1983)*

"SO FAR SO GOOD" were always the first words
out of my father-in-law's mouth whenever I asked him
how he was doing. Those words truly described Mecys'
positive attitude and how he embraced every moment
during the twenty years I knew him. During that time
he was always helping others in his parish, including
performing repairs at friends' homes (he was a trained
carpenter who earlier had worked on major Chicago
high-rises) and driving others to medical appointments,
to church, and to senior centers. He was an avid reader
who continually educated himself on current social and
political issues and the rapidly changing ways of the
world. He was also a tireless chess player—a master in
his own right—who always "took me to school" and
drained me mentally. Mecys was deeply religious and

always open to learning about the beliefs of others. And he rarely failed to exercise for twenty minutes in the morning and before turning in for the evening.

When he was ninety-eight years old, Mecys fulfilled his lifelong dream of moving to California. He adapted quickly to living in an elders' apartment building, where he took up painting, did chair yoga, walked the neighborhood daily, and assisted other residents in a most gentlemanly manner.

Some might say that Mecys's aging gracefully was due to his good genes or luck of the draw. But I believe it was more attributable to his positive outlook on life, compassion for and being of service to others, and love of learning and exploration. He even expressed the desire to visit Jerusalem when he turned one hundred, but when his time came, he accepted death. In his final days, I kiddingly asked him if he wanted to play one more game of chess. He responded with a twinkle in his eye, "Here or over there?" Thus, like Dr. George, Greg, and others whose stories I have shared, by living in acceptance, Mecys was graced with greater joy and serenity.

THE CHALLENGES OF ELDER ACCEPTANCE

The keys to accepting our limitations discussed in the last chapter apply equally with aging. Elders, however, face additional challenges. They must not only deal with the physical and mental setbacks that impact their freedom and independence but also with prevalent societal attitudes and views of their social and economic worth. Elders are more often viewed as a drain on valuable economic and social resources than for the valuable gifts they can provide us. Indeed, instead of seeking and benefiting from elders' well-earned wisdom and life struggles and experiences, we too often bemoan their perceived shortcomings, burdens, and limitations. Still other challenges are presented by having to adapt to the ever-expanding impact of technology in their lives, in which smartphones, social media, apps, a plethora of wireless devices, and such are the norm.

It's no wonder that many people don't look forward to their later years with any sense of joy and happiness. But that need not be, especially for elders who practice acceptance. There is a direct link between elders' acceptance of, and adaptation to, their losses and their quality of life. For example, a study involving 340 adults ranging in age from twenty-one to seventy-three found that older adults are happier than younger ones. Key researcher Iris Mauss, a psychologist and assistant professor at the University of California, Berkeley, noted:

"Acceptance is good for everyone. It just seems to be the case that older people use it more than younger people. They're sort of wise to it."

One reason offered for this was that as people grow old, they experience more life events that are out of their control, such as disease and the death of loved ones, and simply realize that there are more things that they need to accept.[2]

Some call the process of adapting to the profound changes of aging as accepting the "new normal."

ACCEPTING THE NEW NORMAL

Marriage and family therapist Linda Lewis describes the dynamics of the new normal as follows:

"As we age, transitions are increasingly accompanied by feelings of loss, sadness, or decline. . . . Each of these events requires adaptation. We're forced to create a new normal that centers on declining health, moving to a smaller home, leaving behind friendships, quitting activities we've enjoyed, or caring for an ailing spouse."[3]

Denial, anger, and fear make adaptation difficult. We naturally want to hold on to life as it was before and are resentful when we can't. But elders who are willing to accept their new normal are able to make successful life adjustments, as Muriel did.

MURIEL ADAPTS TO HER NEW NORMAL

Muriel Balash had a long and successful career as a documentary film director. However, at age eighty she began losing what she calls "control of her mind" and was fearful the problem would get worse. For example, she would buy something in the store and leave what she bought at the counter. Muriel realized that she needed to learn constructive ways to adapt to her limitations. She now records everything she does in a journal in case she can't remember. She even writes down when she calls someone. Muriel is clear about the need to accept the impairments that come with her memory loss: "[I] accept the fact that there are now limitations that I didn't have before. They don't have to limit life's pleasures, the things that you love to do. . . .There are things you need to adapt to, and you're going to need help."[4]

ACCEPTING THE LOSS OF CONTROL AND INDEPENDENCE

The new normal includes accepting loss of control and independence, perhaps the two most formidable obstacles to satisfaction later in life. Simply put, we can no longer do and enjoy the many things we once could, and that is a real loss. As with other limitations, accepting and grieving these losses is vital to moving beyond them.

Recent research, however, shows that acceptance significantly offsets the impact of loss of control and independence. A study by Deakin University in Australia found that the ability to accept what can't be changed is as important as the feeling of being able to exert control. The study concluded that "in order to protect the well-being of older individuals, adaptation involves both a sense of control and the active acceptance of what cannot be changed. . . . Acceptance takes more of a prime position in low-control situations."

The study took eight key areas of satisfaction into account: standard of living, health, achieving in life, personal relationships, safety, community connectedness, future security, and spirituality and religion.[5]

ELDER ACCEPTANCE STRATEGIES

Now that I am in my mid-seventies, I have a greater awareness that my life journey lessens with each passing year.

Consequently, I try to maintain a deeper (and daily) sense of gratitude for the many blessings in my life—a caring, loving wife and children, overall good health, parents still alive, good friends, and financial security being just a few important ones. Doing so makes me feel more humble and content—and accepting.

Yet I know that the challenges of accepting my age-related limitations and losses will only increase and that to ease the hardship, I must adopt constructive acceptance strategies and practices. Ultimately, I believe such strategies and practices are personal for each of us since we have our own coping mechanisms. Still, I would like to offer some that make a great deal of sense to me based on my readings and research on aging; experiences with, and observations of, other elders like Mecys; recent scientific studies and advances; and lastly, what I have found to be true for me.

CONTINUE TO LEARN

Most elders have the opportunity to expand their learning and educational horizons in ways they were unable to when they were working and raising families. Our time and other constraints are less, and our interests and open-mindedness likely greater. We may even be more adventuresome and curious. In recent years, for example, I have enjoyed a variety of new interests, including birding and nature photography, swimming, meditating, becoming handier around the house, and learning about scientific and technological advancements. I also have had the opportunity to write and blog more, attend and speak at personal growth and recovery meetings and workshops, and counsel and mentor others. In short, for elders who are game and willing, the opportunities for personal growth and learning are considerable and rewarding.

Explore Your Creativity

The creative arts are deeply engrossing and enriching at any age. With more time and less pressure, elders have a unique opportunity to explore their creativity, even if they haven't done so in the past or feel they aren't any good at it. Pure and simple, I have found that creative endeavors lift our spirits and soothe our hearts.

I believe that is the reason many elders sketch, draw, and have fun with coloring books. Many also sing and enjoy chess, card games, crossword puzzles, and other activities. New hobbies can also be pursued, such as Mecys did in taking up painting and chair yoga, and Karl in chapter 2 did in becoming a photography teacher.

I found that I am much more creative now than earlier in my life. I am freer, more patient, and much less judgmental. I am able to let go of more control, trust my instincts, and enjoy the creative process. As a result, when I took up oil painting, to my pleasant surprise, in a short time I was painting appealing landscapes, still lifes, and portraits—this after many years of strongly believing I had no artistic talent. I also began composing poems based on memorable life events of loved ones and subjects of importance to me. (Some of my paintings and poems can be viewed at my website, www.danielamiller.com.)

I encourage you to explore your own creativity. You will find that it centers and grounds you and brings healing light to your life—light that can alleviate pain and suffering. And you are never too old to do it. The famous abstract artist, Willem de Kooning, painted museum quality paintings well into his nineties, even with Alzheimer's disease. You can start with simple creative endeavors, sitting outdoors and sketching flowers and trees on a pad, for instance. I enjoy planting and arranging succulents inside palm fronds from my yard's palm trees and then adding small seashells and colorful rocks.

EXERCISE DAILY

It is well proven that regular exercise is good for both mind and body. It can be anything you're able to do, as long as you do it on a regular basis. Neighborhood walks, working out in a gym, swimming, light yoga, and simply stretching are all good ways to exercise.

We, of course, will need to make adjustments with time, as I did with my tennis. And let's not forget Dr. George in the last chapter, who enjoyed hitting tennis balls even with a portable oxygen tank attached to his back. I am personally inspired by my dad, who at ninety-five still hits golf balls at the driving range and works out at the gym when the weather is too hot, and by my mom, now ninety-three, who hasn't let a debilitating stroke prevent her from exercising several times a week at a physical therapy facility.

SHARE YOUR WISDOM

A blessing of old age is the wisdom we gain through our multitude of life experiences, trials and tribulations, and successes and failures. Not only do these insights and wisdom make our own lives fuller and more content, but sharing them with others, particularly the young, is a wonderful gift for them. Sharing can be in the form of mentoring, teaching, writing, and speaking.

It has long been considered a universal truth that the more we give, the more we receive—be it gratification, stimulation, or social interaction. With much more time available to them, elders are uniquely positioned to be of service to others. Many volunteer at libraries, museums, religious organizations, and such. Others read to other elders who no longer are able, assist with their medicine protocol, make phone calls for them, communicate with their families, and include them in social activities, as well as provide encouragement, moral support, and listen attentively to their concerns. And certainly warm greetings and friendly smiles go a long way.

The benefits of the kinds of activities, engagements, and involvements referenced above were confirmed in a study involving qualitative interviews of elders, sponsored in part by the National Institute of Mental Health, the Department of Veterans Affairs, and the Sam and Rose Stein Institute for Research on Aging at the University of California, San Diego. The study found that 95 percent of the participants felt that remaining engaged with life and self-growth was instrumental to successful aging. Here are what some elders expressed:

"You can't always do the things you did do, but there are other things you can do. . . ."

"I think it really helps me to feel there's another challenge ahead—a couple of challenges. I wish I'd live another 20 years."

"I feel that every social interaction that I have is always a learning process. There are so many people who have had experiences that I can glean from . . . I can get their knowledge and I can incorporate it into myself and that's growing."[6]

CREATION OF NEW BRAIN CELLS

These kinds of activities and involvements are not only beneficial to elders in and of themselves. They also create new brain cells!

It's long been known that we lose brain cells as we age. The good news is that we now know that they can be replaced with new ones. Dr. Amar Sahay, a neuroscientist with Harvard-affiliated Massachusetts General Hospital, relates, "The dogma for the longest time was that adult brains couldn't generate any new brain cells. You just use what you were born with. . . . But the reality is that everyone has the capacity to develop new cells that can help enhance cognitive functions."

The process is called *neurogenesis,* in which new neurons (brain cells) develop in the hippocampus region of the brain, which is responsible for learning information, storing long-term memories, and regulating emotions. Recent studies indicate that adults produce seven hundred new neurons per day, and by the time we turn fifty, we will have exchanged the neurons we were born with in that part of the brain with adult-generated neurons.

Neurogenesis is enhanced through the practice of Neurobics, which are brain exercises aimed at stimulating the five senses in unexpected ways. The term *neurobics* was coined by Dr. Lawrence Katz, a professor of neurobiology at Duke University Medical Center. Dr. Katz says, "Just like aerobic exercises emphasize different muscle groups to enhance coordination and flexibility, neurobic exercises involve activating many different brain areas to increase the range of mental motion." As a consequence, he says, the mind is better fit to meet mental challenges like learning a computer program, remembering names, and staying creative in work.

These exercises include changing your regular routines, such as using your nondominant hand to brush your teeth or stir your coffee, changing where you eat, varying your daily schedule, and such. Dr. Sahay says that it can be anything "that makes you concentrate more on the task. . . . Even engaging in conversations and reading about new topics help."

Regular exercise is also a mainstay of cell growth. Further, neuroscientist Dr. Sandrine Thuret says that new neurons are also created by a diet that includes a high intake of flavonoids, which are contained in dark chocolate, blueberries, and omega-3 fatty acids present in fatty fish like salmon. Conversely, she says, a diet rich in high saturated fat will have a negative impact on neurogenesis.[7]

Elder Spiritual Acceptance

In difficult times, people have long sought comfort by connecting with a divine source or presence in their lives through prayer, religious practices and rituals (formal and informal), meditation, and other means. While elders may have less independence and control over their lives, most can still pursue and benefit from spiritual paths.

As I mentioned previously, the Serenity Prayer is my primary acceptance guide and no less so with respect to accepting the limitations of getting older. I believe this prayer encompasses what many researchers, studies, and gerontologists have found to be instrumental in successful aging.

Accepting the Things We Cannot Change

When we are more accepting of the things we no longer can change or control, we will despair less and thus have more serenity in our lives. As one interviewee in the qualitative interview study said:

"Successful aging is accepting what you are at this time. Not dwelling on what you could have been or forgot to do or couldn't do or things you want to do that you are no longer capable of."

When we dwell on our losses, it obscures the choices and opportunities we do have to make our lives better. John Schappi's inspiring story that follows is an example of how accepting adversity allows us to focus on the meaningful things we can still accomplish.

COURAGE TO CHANGE THE THINGS WE CAN

John was diagnosed with Parkinson's disease in 2009, when he was eighty, which brought with it the fear of dementia. As a means of connecting with others and sharing his "experience, strength, and hope," he started a blog, *Aging and Parkinson's and Me*. In particular, John focused on applying the Serenity Prayer to reduce his fears. He began by identifying the non-changeable risk factors that he learned could lead to dementia and that he needed to accept:

- He was over seventy years of age.
- There was a family history of dementia.
- He had Parkinson's disease.
- He had a low educational level and socioeconomic status.

He next identified the following adverse health factors in his life over which he felt he had some control:

- High blood pressure and cholesterol.
- Smoking and alcohol consumption.
- Depression.

John then identified the positive lifestyle changes he had the power to make (the "courage to change the things he could"):

- Exercise regularly.
- Remain socially connected.
- Keep mentally engaged and challenged.
- Get regular and restful sleep.
- Maintain a brain-healthy Mediterranean diet.

Five years later and nearing eighty-seven, John once again realized that he needed to accept and adapt to the inevitable worsening of his progressive disease, foremost of which was conserving his increasingly limited energy. He thus cancelled his daily delivery of the *Washington Post* and now gets only the Sunday newspaper; he threw out 90 percent of the books he had stashed all over the house, as well as his overflowing recycling bin of papers and printouts he no longer needed; and he stopped researching and writing long blog posts about general health issues and instead wrote much shorter blog posts limited to Parkinson's health matters.

John says that the change was a win-win for him because the posts were quicker and easier for him to do, and he spent less time at the computer, which was one of his goals.[8]

ACCEPTANCE AND FEAR OF DYING

It is my belief that the more we fear death, the more difficult it will be for us to accept the losses of getting older without undue despair. We will be too preoccupied with what we no longer can do rather than the rewarding things that are available to us. We will also be prone to thinking and viewing things negatively instead of positively. On the other hand, when we are able to view death as a natural part of the life cycle—simply an aspect of life's impermanence—and don't fear it, we will live more in the moment and have a greater awareness of the many things that can still bring us joy.

Maintaining Purpose and Meaning in Our Lives

If I had to say what is most important for me at this point in my life, it would be continuing to find purpose in it, an ongoing sense of meaning and worth, and knowing that I can hopefully contribute something of value to others. In fact, I think we all have a desire to feel we are leading a meaningful life. Certainly writing, mentoring, enjoying creative endeavors, playing tennis, practicing gratitude and acceptance, and maintaining close and loving bonds with my family and loved ones have brought me a great deal of personal satisfaction.

I strongly believe that the more elders are able to maintain a sense of purpose and meaning in their lives through doing whatever brings them that, the easier it will be for them to accept their losses and limitations. They may be retired from their jobs, but they don't have to be "retired" from leading a purposeful and meaningful life. I am confident John Schappi would tell us that establishing and contributing to his Parkinson's blog brings tremendous meaning and satisfaction to his life, despite his worsening condition.

Elder Acceptance Intentions

Today I will

Try something new or different.
Not dwell on what I can no longer do.

Be sure to exercise.
Appreciate what I can still do and enjoy.
Share what I have learned with others.
Change my normal routines.
Do something creative.
Be of service to others.
Be grateful for the blessings in my life.

Not all losses and setbacks are physical or mental in nature. Setbacks, losses, and failures occur in all aspects of our lives, including work, financial, social—even educational, as we will see in the next chapter.

CHAPTER FIFTEEN

ACCEPTING SETBACKS AND FAILURE

Our greatest glory is not in never failing,
but in rising up every time we fail.

—*Oliver Goldsmith*[1]

BECCA MADE THE DEAN'S list each semester during her first two years of college and was also awarded an academic scholarship. No surprise really; she was smart, skilled, and knew how to study effectively. However, after transferring schools before her junior year, a series of traumatic events derailed everything for her. The chaos triggered a major depressive episode. Too depressed and heartbroken to get out of bed most days, she began missing classes and failed to turn in important papers. Consequently, she failed almost every class, jeopardizing her scholarship.

Becca felt she had failed herself and every person who had believed in her along the way. She began seeing a therapist to help with her depression and the events that triggered it and was encouraged to keep trying. She managed to graduate, but she just barely passed certain classes and had to retake others. In her words, "I didn't triumphantly race across the finish line to graduation— I limped, precariously close to giving up even at the very end."

Two years following graduation, Becca had a far different perspective about the nature of failure and the hidden blessings in accepting it, as she shares:

"I would not relive that time willingly. But there is something I learned from failing for two years straight; I learned the art of *accepting* my failure, moving on, and trying again. . . . Failure is a vital part of existence, one that will always be a possibility on the horizon. Facing it, accepting it, nursing your wounds, and getting back up again—that's the thing that makes you stronger."[2]

Becca's story is powerful. She learned to move forward with her life with grace, strength, and acceptance.

THE BLESSINGS OF FAILURE

There are other benefits of failure. Let's take a look at some of them.

INDELIBLE LIFE LESSONS

The very pain and agony of failure not only motivates us to do better in the future but, just as importantly, it teaches us valuable life lessons—perhaps better than through any other means. A case in point is the lesson I learned in the finals of a seniors' tennis tournament. After I had jumped to a 4–1 lead, my opponent became nervous and double-faulted the first point of the next game and I soon had a 30–15 lead. However, instead of staying in the moment, I mentally jumped ahead to my winning the game and serving out the set with a commanding 5–1 lead. Of course that's not what happened. I played the next point too casually and lost it— and also the next two points and game. With renewed confidence, my opponent then started banging the ball, taking me out of my game, and won ten of the next eleven games and the match!

I was very disheartened and felt like a total failure. For the next twenty-four hours I kept replaying key points in my mind, causing myself to have a sleep-deprived night.

Fortunately, by the next day I was able to forgive myself and accept my failure by reminding myself that I simply had a bad day and that a bad day didn't mean a bad life—or that I was a bad player! This better perspective brought an end to the self-torment. Just as importantly, with that acceptance, I saw very clearly what I needed to do the next time I was in a similar situation; namely, stay focused and in the present moment, play one point at a time, and continue playing the same way that had given me the lead.

To benefit the most from failure, I don't feel we should forgive and forget. Rather, we should *accept* and *learn*. By that I mean, just as with my tennis story, we should try to ascertain the specific reasons why we failed so that we can avoid making the same mistakes going forward. We should consider such things as whether we were too optimistic, or weren't diligent enough, or that our expectations were too high, or that we simply took on too much.

BREEDING SUCCESS

Michael Jordan, widely considered the best basketball player of all time, explains how his failures were responsible for his success as a basketball player:

"Look, I've missed more than 9,000 shots in my career, I've lost 300 games; twenty-six times I've taken the game-winning shot and missed. I've failed over and over again in my life and that's why I succeeded."[3]

So too, does famed motivational author Napoleon Hill:

"Every adversity, every failure and every unpleasant experience carries with it the seed of an equivalent benefit which may prove a blessing in disguise."[4]

GREATER RESILIENCY

As Becca's story illustrates, failure provides us with an opportunity to pick ourselves up again and move forward in a more positive manner. It makes you stronger and better prepared to handle life's constant ups and downs. In short, you become more resilient, and as you do, you gain a better sense of who you are and what you are capable of doing. You become a survivor, and knowing that allows you to more easily work through the fears and anxiety of future endeavors, making success more probable. Without failure, you would not have these life-changing opportunities.

GREATER HUMILITY

Failure can be very humbling. Some people are brought to their knees. But the pain of failure is not necessarily a bad thing. Through it, we realize we are not so all knowing or mistake free as we often fool ourselves into believing. Failure gives us the humility to be more open-minded and willing to listen to others. It also allows us to reexamine our attitudes and our lives in a clearer light. And with greater humility, we are less likely to fail in the future.

Before taking a look at how we can better accept failure and avail ourselves of its blessings, it is instructive to have a clear understanding of what failure is— and isn't.

DEFINING FAILURE

Failure generally presupposes that we failed at something or didn't perform well enough. It often involves a telling mistake, miscalculation, or oversight. It also is a judgment. But who is the judge of whether we in fact failed? Most commonly it is we ourselves, but it can also be others such as employers, parents, teachers, and the like. But what if we in fact didn't fail? In Becca's case, for example, a reasonable argument can be made that she didn't fail since her perceived "failures" were the result of external events (very likely over which she had little or no control) that impacted her emotional well-being and not because of something she did or didn't do.

Indeed, some believe there is no such thing as failure, but rather the perceived failure is simply part of natural life events and experiences, most of which we have little or no control over. This conforms to the idea of impermanence discussed in chapter 13, in which the flow of life is not predictable and is always changing. Hence, what we may consider failure is only (and simply) part of this natural ebb and flow, and as such, is neither negative nor positive, but simply neutral.

Consequently, we shouldn't too quickly conclude that we have failed. Perhaps we are judging ourselves too harshly. In fact, maybe we're just having a bad day.

IT'S OKAY TO HAVE A BAD DAY!

Dr. Allison Belger, a former master CrossFit competitor with a doctorate in clinical psychology, tells the story about a longtime CrossFit competitor who obsessed for days because his performance standards were far worse than they were a year before. She wondered why instead of feeling like a failure, this athlete couldn't just accept that he had a bad day and that it's part of being human—and life. In explaining the importance of this distinction, she writes:

"If we torture ourselves every time we don't perform as well as we'd hoped, development is also unlikely to unfold. Take the guy from our gym who, at least momentarily, interpreted his performance as an indication that he is less fit and skilled than he was a year ago, despite his training efforts. If he were to allow himself to get stuck there, he might become less and less likely to train hard. Why? Because what's the point of training hard when the results are crap? What's the point of going to the gym week after week when it's apparent that his fitness and competencies have declined? We can see how becoming too invested in the big meaning of a single failure is a slippery slope to throwing in the towel. On the other hand, accepting the reality of bad days would allow this athlete to let it go, have faith in his training, reclaim rational thinking, and

acknowledge he is fitter, more skilled, and more ener-
getic than he was a year ago when we probably tested
his fitness on a 'good' day."[5]

Still, I suspect for most people it is the belief or
feeling of having failed as much as whether they truly
did that is the determinative factor that needs to be addressed—and accepted—in order to avoid remaining in
the abyss of unprocessed failure.

KEYS TO ACCEPTING FAILURE

Let's look at some ways that can help us accept and
embrace failure, whether real or just perceived.

WELCOME TO THE "FAILURE" CLUB

Realizing that almost everyone has failed at some
point in his life gives us a better perspective about
failure: it need not be the end-all or define who we
are or what we are capable of doing. Knowing that
our best and brightest have failed at different points in
their lives helps dampen the sometimes self-scorching
flames of failure. Michael Jordan certainly is not the
only known member of this exclusive club. Here are a
few others:

- Albert Einstein didn't speak fluently until he
  was nine years old. He was expelled from school
  and initially refused admission to the Zurich
  Polytechnic School. He was a mere patent clerk
  when he formulated the general theory of relativ-
  ity that changed the world forever and later won
  the Nobel Prize in science.

- Oprah Winfrey was demoted in her first television job before hosting a highly popular talk show that went on for twenty-five years and becoming the queen of her own media empire.

- Fred Astaire, after taking his first screen test, was evaluated by a studio pro as such: "Can't act. Can't sing. Balding. Can dance a little." He went on to sing, dance, and act his way to stardom through major musicals such as *Top Hat* (1935) and *Shall We Dance* (1937).

- Arianna Huffington, powerful businesswoman and prolific author, had thirty-six publishers reject her second book. Not discouraged, she said, "You can recognize very often that out of these projects that may not have succeeded themselves that other successes are built."

- Steve Jobs dropped out of Oregon's Reed College after one semester and quit his first job before he went on to make Apple the world's largest technology company.

- J. K. Rowling was a struggling single mother on welfare and faced numerous rejections from publishers before going on to write the record breaking Harry Potter book series that later resulted in huge box office film successes.

Consequently, I don't think it would be an overstatement to say, "Failure? What's the big deal?" That is, unless you allow it to be. Let's examine the likely mind-sets of these and others who have used failure as a stepping-stone to later success.

PROCESS YOUR FAILURE

While I feel that it is important to move beyond our failures, we shouldn't try to block or avoid the discomfiting feelings associated with them. To the contrary, it is important to "lean into" such feelings, whether they are anger, fear, shame, or the like, and not try to justify or rationalize what happened. At the same time, however, we shouldn't dwell on them for too long, for that can result in self-pity and despair. I call all this "processing the failure." It allows us to embrace failure and its indelible life lessons—without castigating ourselves. In that manner, we can more readily make necessary adjustments as we pursue new endeavors and opportunities. For me, that is how failure best breeds success.

DON'T MAKE IT PERSONAL

It's important to separate the act of failure from the person. It's not unlike how we view the child who misbehaves. We don't say the child is bad, but rather that the child *acted* badly. Blogger and *Forbes* journalist Susan Tardanico expresses this important distinction this way:

"Separate the failure from your identity. Just because you haven't found a successful way of doing something yet doesn't mean *you are a failure*. . . . These are completely separate thoughts."

To emphasize her point, she tells the story of a man who failed at business when he was twenty-one years old and was defeated in a state legislative race at age twenty-two. He overcame the death of his fiancée at twenty-six and then had a nervous breakdown when he was twenty-seven. Still not deterred, he lost a congressional race at thirty-four, followed by a loss in a senatorial race at forty-five. He failed to become vice president at age forty-seven and lost still another senatorial race at forty-nine. Notwithstanding these setbacks, he was elected President of the United States at the age of fifty-two.[6]

Fortunately for us and our country, Abraham Lincoln didn't take his failures personally! You shouldn't either.

REEXAMINE YOUR EXPECTATIONS

Our sense of failure may be due to initially having unrealistic expectations. We naturally want to be motivated to work hard and "stretch"; however, if we set the bar too high, failure becomes anything short of it. If we see that our expectations were unrealistic, failure becomes less about what we did or didn't do and more about what we should do the next time.

For example, if you volunteered to organize your child's school's annual fund-raiser and your enthusiasm led you to establish an unrealistically high funding goal, not reaching it would not only be disappointing, but you would likely feel that you failed. However, the failure might not be not meeting your financial target but rather your setting your expectations too high in the first place, based on the existing circumstances. Maybe it was the first time you had headed a major fund-raising effort and you weren't familiar with the myriad tasks and coordinated efforts required for a successful event. Perhaps the economy was weak, and therefore donations were smaller. Or maybe the school simply had too many fund-raisers during the year. Hence, whenever you feel that you have failed, you should reexamine your expectations to determine if they were warranted yet be careful not to justify your mistakes or blame them on other people or things.

FORGIVE YOURSELF

In the past, perfection and doing things right was very important to me. It was one of the reasons I was such a big controller. I was afraid of failure, and it didn't take much to make me feel I had failed. I found it very difficult to forgive myself for my errors and mistakes. Instead of accepting them as part of life, I constantly dwelled on them, and that only made me stress—and control—more.

I have since learned that self-forgiveness releases the pressure and heavy burden many of us impose on ourselves. When we no longer dwell on what can't be changed and focus on making effective adjustments going forward, we have less anxiety and more serenity. Now, as long as I feel I made a good-faith effort to succeed, I am able to forgive myself when I make a mistake or fail at something. At work, I accept my mistakes as a natural part of doing business and no longer berate myself. I remain grateful for my overall business acumen and judgment, and that gives me a balanced perspective. If I err at home or in my personal affairs, I promptly try to make appropriate amends to those I have harmed. On the courts, I don't dwell on my "blunders" during a match. I know that if I fret about the last point, I will likely lose the current one. In fact, after an error, I sometimes say to myself "Danny, I forgive you," which immediately lightens my spirit and lets me focus on the next point. I now accept that mistakes are simply part of the game (and life) and I am not, and will never be, a perfect tennis player—or person—what a relief!

INTENTIONS FOR ACCEPTING FAILURE

If I feel I have failed at something, I will

Not take it too personally.
Identify what I have learned from the experience.
Reexamine my original expectations.
Remember that I am not perfect.
Lean in to my painful feelings.
Separate the failure from who I am.
Forgive myself!

We have so far explored instructive ways in which we can better accept others and things as they are. But what about accepting what is perhaps the most complex and challenging person in our lives: ourselves! The next part looks at some ways we can better accept ourselves.

PART IV

ACCEPTING OURSELVES

CHAPTER SIXTEEN

TRUTHS AND PARADOXES OF SELF-ACCEPTANCE

The worst loneliness is not to be comfortable with yourself.

—*Mark Twain*

MIKE STRUGGLED WITH BEING a people pleaser through most of his adult life. He felt like a chameleon, always expressing what others wanted to hear rather than how he really felt about things. He judged himself harshly because of it. After a lot of introspection, he better understood what he needed to do to change his ways. In Mike's words,

"I became very clear about my people-pleasing tendencies and why I was that way. I needed approval from others because as a kid, my parents told me I was never good enough. I heard it so much, I believed it well into my adult life. I felt what I believed wasn't valid or important, certainly not to others. So I feared expressing it. I didn't want to be put down. People's approval was too important to me. But I never liked being that way.

203

I knew for sure that any change had to come from me, and that blaming others did absolutely no good. Pure and simple, I knew I had to drum up the courage to express how I truly felt about things, without fearing rejection or adverse reaction.

"It wasn't easy, to be sure. It was very difficult in the beginning. I often felt shaky and my voice was unsteady. For the most part, though, the responses weren't nearly as strong as I had feared; many people even concurred with my views. Gradually I felt more confident and less fearful in expressing them. The risk of someone rejecting or not liking me didn't hold me back as it did before. The people-pleasing part of me still crops up at times, but much less so than before. I now accept that it is simply a part of me, without judging myself. It's just who I am and I'm now okay with that."

Unlike the stories shared in previous chapters where people struggled with having to accept unalterable conditions, Mike's story is an example of the type of negative mental state or attitude or behavior that we do have the power to change or improve. These traits are sometimes harshly referred to as personality or character defects or flaws. I prefer to call them shortcomings, since that lessens the tendency toward self-judgment.

Being able to accept these characteristics of ourselves not only results in a greater sense of peacefulness but, importantly, also enables us to more readily accept them in others as well. A primary focus of this and the next chapter will be on accepting and improving upon our shortcomings as an integral part of being able to accept ourselves more fully and enjoy the blessings that follow. But first, let's examine what self-acceptance means.

THE MEANING OF SELF-ACCEPTANCE

Self-acceptance, as I mean it, is the acceptance of ourselves as we are—both the good and the bad—*without* self-judgment. To that, I would add, "and without harboring negative feelings about ourselves—in particular, guilt and shame." As such, it is the acknowledgment of who and what we are without adornment.

For me, it more simply means being comfortable with myself as I am, or as some would say, in my own skin. Twenty years ago, for the most part, I was not. Now, for the most part, I am. The process I followed is essentially twofold. First, I needed to know myself more fully. Second, I needed to accept who I was without self-judgment or negative feelings, which in my case required making the necessary changes or improvements until I could. As I explain in the next chapter, I did this through doing a personal accounting of my ways and then making a concerted effort to improve upon those ways that didn't serve me well. This all may seem very basic. However, there are several inherent paradoxes in the process of self-acceptance that make it more complex.

THE PARADOXES OF SELF-ACCEPTANCE

One paradox is that in learning more about ourselves, we will likely discover certain traits—maybe even secrets—that we don't like or feel comfortable with, potentially making self-acceptance more fleeting than before. To avoid judging or having negative feelings about these things, some people may need to make a concerted effort to change or improve upon their limitations. However, at this point, another paradox may arise, namely, that we may need to first accept ourselves as we are—blemishes and all—before we can proceed to make the improvements we want. The view here is that everyone is imperfect and that accepting our imperfections should be the main priority and goal. Simply stated, *we* are enough. However, this in turn may subject us to another paradox: if we accept ourselves, imperfections and all—*without* any efforts toward self-improvement—we may be prone to becoming complacent, thereby impeding further personal growth.

So which is it? All of the above? Some of the above? None of the above? These are intriguing questions and each finds support in the many writings on the subject. Once again, however, in this very tricky and complex area of our lives, in a general sense, the answers most likely lie in "the space between." More specifically, I believe that it ultimately depends on one's unique nature and makeup and that each of us will readily discover which method or methods works best.

Moreover, you will likely find, as I did, that it helps at times to switch from one method to another, depending on the particular traits you are dealing with. Some character traits are more debilitating than others. For example, some people I know (including me) were constantly undermined by volatile rage and anger—to the point where they had a lot of despair and little serenity. Their ability to accept themselves depended upon their making a concerted effort to become more aware of the things that triggered their flashes of anger (typically fear, lack of control, high expectations, and the need to be perfect) and then working hard at moderating those feelings and attitudes.

Since so much of the process is personal, I will share with you how I navigated to a more complete acceptance of myself in the hope that it will be of assistance in your quest for self-acceptance. I began with this fundamental inquiry: Can I ever fully accept myself? My answer was no. That said, it did not discourage me from taking little steps toward greater self-acceptance. That seemed to me a more realistic and achievable goal and avoided the "trying too hard" and "self-judging" syndromes that easily impede us. Moreover, the quest for self-acceptance has less pressure—and quite likely enjoyment, and even elation—if we view the journey in terms of progress and not perfection.

IMPORTANT TRUTHS ABOUT SELF-ACCEPTANCE

I believe that there are certain innate "truths" about self-acceptance:

- *It will come and go, depending on the circumstances and how we feel in the moment.* Life's constant, unexpected swings will always create challenges that can impact us emotionally, spiritually, financially, and physically. It may be a feeling of failure or loss or a misstep; perhaps it's being criticized or rejected by someone or raging uncontrollably about something. Momentarily,

208 | THE GIFTS OF ACCEPTANCE

at least, we may judge ourselves harshly and get down on ourselves, even in self-pity and thus not be accepting of ourselves. When that happens to me, I try to "lean into" and address my fears, anger, pains, and discomforts and remember that I am resilient enough to survive and that tomorrow will be a new day. I also try to be cognizant of my personal qualities and grateful for the many blessings I have—and accept that all are part of life's impermanence.

- *It is a lifelong pursuit.* As mentioned previously, the road to self-acceptance will have bumps and U-turns—and even some roadblocks—but as long as we are patient, willing, and grateful for our progress, more rewards lie ahead of us. My journey is increasingly more rewarding—even exciting at times—as I become more and more comfortable with who I am. I am confident that the same will be true for you as well.

- *It will always be impacted by our shortcomings.* With the willingness and commitment to improve our lives, our limitations and shortcomings will diminish and be less impactful over time. However, they rarely leave us entirely. They can unexpectedly or unintentionally arise from outside events or influences, impeding our self-acceptance, at least temporarily. What is important is that we avoid self-judgment and that we respond to our limitations and shortcomings in a manner that diminishes their impact.

CATALYSTS FOR
SELF-ACCEPTANCE

The following mind-sets and practices promote self-acceptance:

- *Awareness.* Awareness is a prerequisite to acceptance. We must learn with clarity—and without denial or self-justification—the things we need to accept about ourselves, both good and bad. A personal accounting explained in the next chapter is an effective way to gain such awareness.

- *Self-forgiveness and self-compassion.* Since we are not perfect and never will be, we need to honor that by being compassionate and forgiving of ourselves—which is to say, of our failures, our missteps, and our faults. When we don't, we become mired in guilt and shame, always judging ourselves. Eighteenth-century English poet Alexander Pope expresses it well in *An Essay on Criticism:* "To err is human, to forgive Divine."

- *Rejection of our "inner critic."* Many of us are easily undermined by our "inner critic," that little voice within us that constantly tells us that we're doing things wrong, we're not good or nice enough, we've failed again, we don't have what it takes, our future is dim, and the myriad other mistruths. You may not be aware of how incessant this voice is. Take a minute—just one—and listen to it, and you will readily see what I mean.

The remedy for this internal "pest" is clear. We need to hush it the best we can. This can be extremely difficult, however, if you have a very active mind like me. I suppose that being a hyperactive thinker, strategizer, and planner helped me achieve business and financial success, but the constant chatter that entails also led to many sleepless nights filled with fears, anxieties, and worst-case scenarios.

Being more compassionate and accepting of myself did a lot to silence my chatter. I also learned that almost everything my inner critic said was not true and was primarily a by-product—and an unhealthy one at that—of my fears and anxieties. Indeed, it is how these powerful emotions often express themselves. I now recognize that they are mostly illusory (*"False Evidence Appearing Real"* and *"Future Events Already Ruined"*).

Practicing mindfulness or mindful meditation aimed at quieting the mind is also very helpful in disarming the inner critic. When we quiet the mind and stay in the present, we also quiet the critic—or at least let its naysaying pass through our thoughts without incident. Finally, we should always be mindful of our attributes and all the good within us and let them refute the negativity of our inner critic.

- *Commitment to improving our shortcomings.* As mentioned before, I believe that the more we reduce or improve upon our shortcomings, the easier it is to accept ourselves as we are without self-judgment. With diminished shortcomings, there are fewer things that can cause us discomfort.

- *Acceptance of others.* I found that the more I accept others as they are, including their frailties, faults, and idiosyncrasies, the easier it becomes for me to accept my own. When I judge others less, I judge myself less. When I forgive others more readily, I forgive myself more readily. As I see the good in others, I see it more in myself. Hence, being kind, compassionate, and accepting of others allows us to be that way with ourselves.

Constantly taking account of and applying these truths and catalysts provides us with a better and more balanced perspective of what the journey of self-acceptance involves. It removes the pressure of trying to be perfect. It allows us to look forward to our journey of self-discovery and self-acceptance with confidence and safety, knowing that the gifts and blessings of acceptance await us along the way.

Let's now see how we can learn more about ourselves, which is to say, let's find out more who we *truly* are!

CHAPTER SEVENTEEN

DISCOVERING AND ACCEPTING WHO WE ARE

The privilege of a lifetime is being who you are.
—*Joseph Campbell,* A Joseph Campbell Companion:
Reflections on the Art of Living

THE JULY 1 READING from *Courage to Change,* an Al-Anon Family Groups daily reader, puts the journey of self-acceptance in a healthy perspective:

"Most of us have spent far too much time feeling badly about who we are and what we have done. Others may have harshly criticized us or we may have simply lost perspective and become overly hard on ourselves. . . . It takes time for old doubts to fade and wounds to heal. Self-confidence comes slowly, but it grows with practice. We can begin by acknowledging that we do have positive qualities. . . . For every defect we identify, we can also try to name an asset."[1]

The journey toward discovering and understanding one's true "self" is a lifelong, uneven one, marked by both exciting insights and discouraging setbacks.

Yet, ultimately, it is highly rewarding. Therapy, counseling, meditation, journaling, and reflecting on past experiences and struggles are all common facilitators. Whatever methods and choices you make, it is important that you give due consideration to your positive traits or qualities in order to have a balanced and "whole" perspective of yourself. It is also important to shed light on your denial of your positive attributes and of your shortcomings. Make it a rigorously honest and probing endeavor. If there is discomfort, it likely means you are digging beneath the surface and discovering vital things about yourself.

THE SKIN TEST

Before I made a concerted effort at self-examination I thought I knew my pros and cons pretty well. That turned out not to be the case. I suspect that may be the same for you. As you begin your self-discovery process, try to get an overall sense of how comfortable you feel about the way you are. One way you can do this is by asking yourself this core question or one like it: *Am I comfortable in my own skin?* Yes? No? Not sure? Whatever you believe, take a "skin test" to get a better idea. The one that follows is drawn from both my experiences and those of others I know or have mentored. You should personalize, modify, and add to it as you see fit.

In answering the questions that follow, the main consideration is whether you have the *propensity* to feel or be the ways described.

Do you try to please others?

Do you often feel guilty?
Do you tend to take things too personally?
Do you try to impress others?
Do you need or seek accolades from others?
Are you overly concerned about what others think or say about you?
Are you easily shamed?
Are you too often a "doormat?"
Are you reluctant to express contrary views?

"Yes" answers to a number of these questions may indicate that you have some discomfort or insecurities about the way you are or act—at least in certain realms of your life.

Now answer these questions:

Do you handle criticism well?
Are you comfortable expressing contrary views?
Do you let go of your failures?
Do you stand up for yourself?
Do you take proper care of your personal needs?
Are you comfortable saying no to others?
Do you like yourself?

Answering "yes" to these questions is an indication that you're comfortable in your own skin, meaning with who you are. There will likely be some "mostlys" or "I'm not sures," which is okay.

What I hope, however, is that this exercise will highlight or identify certain traits or patterns about yourself that are worth exploring further through a personal accounting that follows. Ideally, the goal is to find a balance between extreme patterns of behavior and attitudes that feels right—for *you*.

TAKING A PERSONAL ACCOUNTING

Conducting a personal accounting of your perceived pluses and minuses will provide you with a more inclusive, balanced view of yourself. There are various ways to do a self-assessment. The main requirement is that it be thorough and probing. The fourth step of the 12-step programs describes the task as making *"a searching and fearless moral inventory of ourselves."*

In doing so, consider where you feel you fall short. What things hold you back? What do you like about yourself and what don't you like about yourself? What behavior makes you feel bad or guilty? What would you like to do better? What things no longer serve you well? And so on. It's helpful to refer to a list that identifies a wide variety of personality traits. You can find some by Googling "personality lists." The website Ideonomy has a list of over six hundred traits, separated into positive, neutral, and negative.[2]

You can do your inventory alone, but I highly recommend enlisting the assistance of a trusted friend or family member who can help you flesh out and clarify particular character and personality traits, both positive and negative. Otherwise, you may narrow the scope too much, as well as fall prey to easy rationalizations and self-justifications. A third party will also be more neutral and objective and help you delve deeper when you may have some reluctance, as well as be supportive when suppressed emotional issues arise, which is common, or if you are too self-critical.

As you do your personal assessment, you will discover certain positive traits that you were unaware or not fully aware of, such as being kind, generous, cooperative, trusting, forgiving, tolerant, perceptive, open-minded, patient, and nondemanding. It's important to remember that they are vital parts of who you are and you should give them their just due. Many of us try to downplay such qualities. We more easily see what's wrong than right about ourselves. This is not the time to be modest!

IMPROVING OUR SHORTCOMINGS

Your accounting will also reveal traits that are stronger than you believed or that you wish you didn't have, such as being self-indulgent, self-centered, smug, judgmental, critical, selfish, domineering, submissive, lazy, impatient, intolerant, controlling, and so on. These are important truths that will always be a part of us in some form or another. Whether because of genetics, early childhood traumas, or abusive or overbearing parents, they become part of "our constitution." For many of us, they have also become part of our survival mode, providing us with a certain sense of safety and security that we are reluctant to do without. When they no longer serve that purpose, we can begin to let them go. Yet since they are so deeply embedded within us, I believe that it is more feasible and realistic to work toward diminishing their strength and impact, as well as reducing their frequency, as opposed to trying to remove them totally. It's more important that we honor and appreciate our successes than bemoan our setbacks.

Moreover, there is often a fine line between a so-called shortcoming and a personal quality, and we thus need to be careful that we don't change an asset into a liability. In many instances, our assets and liabilities are flip sides of each other. For example, when does confidence become arrogance? When does concern for others become enabling? When does taking care of others lead to lack of self-care? When does ridding fear become throwing caution to the wind? And when does being understanding of others become not standing up for oneself? If we misuse our assets, they can become liabilities. The key is to try to find the proper balance between such opposing forces, which most likely is in "the space between."

APPROACHES TO IMPROVING OUR SHORTCOMINGS

Once you have done your self-assessment, there are several ways you can proceed. You can focus on accepting and feeling comfortable with your limitations as being part of who you are now without concurrently attempting to remove or improve upon them. If you are comfortable with yourself at that point, meaning that you accept yourself—blemishes and all—*without* self-judgment, you need go no further.

Alternatively, you can choose to work on improving your shortcomings as a means of more fully accepting yourself. I chose this latter way because I was uncomfortable with certain shortcomings—particularly my control and anger issues. It was not until I was able to significantly reduce those impediments that I found peace in my life.

There are diverse ways of improving upon your shortcomings. As mentioned before, therapy and counseling are very helpful for many people. Prayer, meditation, and journaling can also help considerably. Others learn from reading personal-growth books, attending self-improvement workshops and seminars, and incorporating spiritual practices into their lives. Many others have achieved positive results from 12-step recovery meetings. These are all very productive and even life-changing endeavors. It's really a matter of which ones work best for you.

These methods and practices are all enhanced by incorporating the following harbingers for positive change.

SHINE THE LIGHT OF AWARENESS

I strongly believe that awareness is the most powerful catalyst for positive change. Greater awareness—whether gained through a personal accounting or other means—of what we want and what we need to change, of what works well for us and what doesn't, and how our shortcomings and missteps impact our lives is hugely significant. Just detecting our shortcomings sooner and noticing when and how they impact us is extremely important.

It's not critical that you know how to or have the wherewithal to change things at the time. Awareness is like a bright, healing light that allows us to repeatedly see how our limitations impact us and others, and that alone eventually leads to positive changes. Depending on the time and circumstances, with greater awareness, we may simply choose to be silent, do nothing in the moment, or possibly disengage from the person or situation. It might also mean expressing our regrets and saying we are sorry or standing up for ourselves and expressing our disapproval. In short, the light of awareness lessens the severity, impact, and frequency of our shortcomings, and it reveals possible solutions and resolutions.

ESTABLISH NEW PATTERNS OF BEHAVIOR

A growing number of neuroscientists believe that our behavior patterns, including our disruptive ones, are implanted within our brain circuits. If this is the case, it makes sense to try to change the negative behaviors by replacing them with positive ones.

So how can we do this? One way is to develop healthier patterns of behavior. Some refer to this as "taking contrary action," which means acting in the opposite manner. Hence, if we are too judgmental of others, we can strive toward being more open-minded. If we are easily put off by others, we can try to be more understanding of them by seeing them through their lens. If we are hurried and impatient, we can practice being more patient. If we are too fearful about certain things, we can try to be more courageous. If we are too controlling, we can loosen the reins. The idea is that constantly repeating the new behavior will eventually override the bad behavior. Ideally, with a lot of practice, the new behavior will become our default mode.

Some people try to modify their behavioral patterns by acting "as if." From doing a personal accounting, I gained a better understanding of my extreme discomfort in certain social and professional settings, particularly when I was among strangers or people I didn't know well. *Reserved* or *introverted* best describes that part of me. As a young child, I tended to isolate and that carried over to my personal and work lives. My employees at one time humorously referred to me as "the brain in the closet." Some people thought I was unfriendly and even smug, which made me feel worse, but I well understood how they could think that. Truth be told, I thought that of others who were like me!

I also saw more clearly how this deprived me of the connection and enjoyment that come with social engagement and interaction with others. Through the years, I tried to overcome my shyness but had little success until I heard several people talk about how acting as they would like to be helped them overcome their former ways. They called it acting "as if." I've also heard it referred to as "fake it until you make it."

In my case, that meant acting as if I were an engaging, outgoing person. At first, the idea of it felt so strange, I had to laugh! (I still do whenever I think about it.) Nonetheless, I drummed up the courage to give it a try. My first attempt at it was to walk all around our neighborhood and say hello to everyone I saw and ask how they were doing. Neighbors, workers, gardeners—everyone. The first several encounters felt strange and unnatural to me. But to my pleasant surprise, almost every person responded with a smile on his or her face.

It was as if my acknowledging them brought them a modicum of joy. What a great feeling that was! The last few blocks of my short journey were easy going and a lot of fun.

I then began reaching out to people in other settings and situations, with similarly positive results. I made new friends, had interesting conversations, and felt a certain ease I hadn't experienced before. To this day, it can still be a stretch for me but a much shorter one because I know the benefits that result.

CONTINUING THE JOURNEY TO SELF-ACCEPTANCE

As noted, I have touched upon self-acceptance primarily from the perspective of what's worked well for me and others I know. Whichever path you choose, I believe the journey to self-acceptance is a lifelong one in which we move closer but never quite reach the destination of complete self-acceptance. It is one that is neither linear nor constant. There will always be ebbs and flows and ups and downs. Know, too, that what works for some may not work for you, and while there is no single or "better" way, the courage to change helps all ways.

I hope this self-inquiry will help you as you journey forward:

What do I need to change or "become" in order to feel better about myself?

I encourage you to envision, reflect, meditate, and write about what these things may be and how doing them might make you feel. Then start doing them.

But do them without expectations. Be open-minded, address any negative feelings or discomfort that arises, and let go of the need to control the outcome. And be grateful for partial successes, viewing setbacks merely as opportunities for further growth.

The Gifts of Acceptance await you!

ACKNOWLEDGMENTS

I wish to acknowledge and thank those who have played instrumental roles in the writing and publication of this book during the past seven years.

My most important thanks go to my loving wife, Sigute, who has supported me in so many ways throughout this endeavor: as a proofreader, reviewer, and constructive critic; as an encourager; and most importantly, as someone who accepts me as I am—annoyances and all. I love and admire you so much, sweetheart!

Thank you also to my wonderful children, Lana, Lora, and Brandon, whose diverse natures and personalities have helped me better practice acceptance as a parent. I cherish the close bond I have with each of you. Thank you, too, to my sister, Suzee, and my parents, Morry and Judy, for their unwavering support and encouragement in my writing endeavors.

I am especially grateful to Sharon Goldinger, whose astute guidance has helped make this a book I am very proud of; Rabbi Beth Lieberman, for her insightful content and organizational recommendations, which made the manuscript more impactful; Mayapriya Long, for her skill and artistry in designing a book cover and interior that convey the sense of peace and serenity that acceptance brings; Rena Copperman, for her good work in copyediting the manuscript; and Chaton Anderson, for her skill and thoroughness in polishing the final manuscript.

I owe a very special thanks to Greg Briscoe, whose grace and courage in living in acceptance under the most difficult of circumstances has inspired me and others in more ways than he may realize.

I also wish to thank Michael Starr and Michael Topp, for their review and constructive comments on important portions of the manuscript, and John MacDonald, Cindy Bloom, Mike Mikane, Ray Grabowski, Jane Hughes, Neil Bucknam, Keith Kim, and Duncan Rayside for sharing their insights and experiences with and about acceptance.

And not without importance, I must thank my "foes" (real and perceived) for providing me the opportunities to also practice acceptance with people who oppose me and thereby make choices that are in my best interest, as opposed to engaging or retaliating to my detriment, as I was prone to do in the past.

Finally, I am grateful to the Al-Anon program and its guiding principles and practices for enhancing my ability to practice acceptance in all my affairs, and to the members of its supportive fellowship for sharing their strength, hope, and experience.

Notes

Introduction

1. Daniel Miller, http://danielamiller.com/.

Chapter 2

1. James Baldwin, "As Much Truth as One Can Bear," *New York Times Book Review*, January 14, 1962.

2. Chris Kresser, "Living with Chronic Illness: The Power of Acceptance," *Chris Kresser* (blog), April 6, 2011, https://chriskresser.com/living-with-chronic-illness -the-power-of-acceptance/.

3. Iva Ursano, "Forgiving Abusive Parents and Setting Ourselves Free," *Tiny Buddha* website, February 2, 2016, http://tinybuddha.com/blog/forgiving-abusive-parents-setting -ourselves-free. (Used with permission of Tiny Buddha.)

4. Marjie Mohtashemi, "Accepting Limits of Old Age Can Ease Fear of Aging," *NY1News*, NY1.com, August 28, 2003, http://www.ny1.com/archives/nyc/all-boroughs/2003/08/28 /accepting-limits-of-old-age-can-ease-fear-of-aging -NYC_32763.old.html (material deleted).

5. Erin Olivo, "Why Acceptance Is One of the Best Stress Reducers," *Psychology Today*, January 2, 2015,

https://www.psychologytoday.com/blog/wise-mind-living
/201501/ why-acceptance-is-one-the-best-stress-reducers.

6. Stephanie Harper, "Learning to Let Go," *Huffington Post,* January 25, 2015, http://www.huffingtonpost.com
/stephanie-harper/learning-to-let-go_1_b_6216296.html.

CHAPTER 3

1. Michael J. Fox, interview by Dotson Rader, "Michael J. Fox at 50: 'I Don't Look at Life as a Battle'," *Parade,* March 29, 2012, https://parade.com/40559/dotsonrader
/michael-j-fox-excerpt/.

2. Donna Torbico, "Acceptance & ACoAs, Part 2," *Heal & Grow for ACoAs,* July 29, 2013, https://acoarecovery.
wordpress.com/2013/07/29/acceptance-acoas-part-2/.

3. Tom Smith, *A Balanced Life: Nine Strategies for Coping with the Mental Health Problems of a Loved One* (Center City, MN: Hazelden, 2008), 74.

4. Marsha Linehan, "Radical Acceptance, Part 1," *DBT* website, http://www.dbtselfhelp.com/html/radical
_acceptance_part_1.html.

CHAPTER 4

1. "Denial and Acceptance (Parkinson's disease)," What
-When-How website, http://what-when-how.com/parkinsons
-disease/denial-and-acceptance-parkinson's-disease/.

CHAPTER 6

1. Thomas Merton, *No Man Is an Island* (Boston: Shambhala, 2005), 177–178.

2. John Burns, "The Way I See It: Accepting Each Other 'As Is,'"*Travelers Rest Tribune,* March 29, 2013.

3. Daniel A. Miller, "Can You Accept Your Loved One's Political Choices?" *Boing Boing* website, October 6, 2016, https://boingboing.net/2016/10/06/can-you-accept-your-loved-one.html

CHAPTER 7

1. University of New Hampshire, "Controlling Parents More Likely to Have Delinquent Children," *Science Daily*, February 10, 2012, https://www.sciencedaily.com/releases/2012/02/120210105901.htm.

2. Sue Shellenbarger, "Ambitious Parents, Mellow Children," *Wall Street Journal*, October 19, 2011, https://www.wsj.com/articles/SB10001424052970204479504576638950410953960.

3. Mitchell Rosen, "Growth Is Key in Parent-Child Relationships," from his October 18, 2014 column in the Riverside Press Enterprise Newspaper, http://www.pe.com/2014/10/18/growth-is-key-in-parent-child-relationships/. (Used with permission of the author.)

4. Kimberly McCafferty, "Never Give Up," *Brick Shorebeat*, March 2, 2015, http://brick.shorebeat.com/2015/03/never-give-up/.

5. Kahlil Gibran, *The Prophet* (New York: Knopf, 1923), 17.

CHAPTER 9

1. Sam Levenson, *Everything but Money: A Life of Riches* (New York: Simon and Schuster, 1966), 163.

2. Keith Gaynor, "How to Cope When You Fall Out with an Adult Sibling," *The Journal.ie,* Dublin, December 22, 2014, http://www.thejournal.ie/readme/adult-sibling-feud-relationships-1772575-Dec2014/.

CHAPTER 10

1. Caroline Chatfield and reader, "We Must Accept Our Friends as They Are," *Deseret News*, April 13, 1937, 16, a syndicated column from the *Kingsport Times*.

2. From *Courage to Change,* page 150, copyright 1992, by Al-Anon Family Group Headquarters, Inc. Reprinted by permission of Al-Anon Family Group Headquarters, Inc. Excerpts from Al-Anon Conference Approved Literature are reprinted with permission of Al-Anon Family Group Headquarters, Inc. Permission to reprint these excerpts does not mean that Al-Anon Family Group Headquarters, Inc. has reviewed or approved the contents of this publication, or that Al-Anon Family Group Headquarters, Inc. necessarily agrees with the views expressed herein. Al-Anon is a program of recovery for family and friends of alcoholics—use of these excerpts in any non Al-Anon context does not imply endorsement or affiliation by Al-Anon.

3. Doug and Ann Termining, "6 Keys to Accepting Others," *Life with Great Friends* (blog), http://lifewithgreatfriends.com/6-keys-to-accepting-others/.

CHAPTER 11

1. Carrie Fisher, *Wishful Drinking* (New York: Simon & Schuster, 2008), 153.

CHAPTER 13

1, Moe Mernick, "How Stuttering Helped Me to Accept and Embrace My Adversities," *Canadian Jewish News,* March 25, 2015, http://www.cjnews.com/perspectives/opinions/stuttering-helped-accept-embrace-adversities.

2. Therese Borchard, "With Depression, Know Your Limits," everydayhealth, http://www.everydayhealth.com

/columns/therese-borchard-sanity-break-with-depression
-know-your-limits/.

3. Gabrielle Blackman-Sheppard, "Brain Response," *Bi-Polar Girl* (blog), http://www.bi-polargirl.com/blogs/gabrielle/brain-response/25-nov-2010.

4. Sarah Hackley, "How Accepting Our Limitations Can Ease the Emotional Pain Associated with Chronic Migraine," *Migraine.com*, February 4, 2015, https://migraine.com/blog/accepting-limitations-can-ease-emotional-pain/. (Used with permission of Health Union, LLC.)

5. Janice Neumann, "Acceptance of Heart Failure Improves Patients' Quality of Life," *Reuters.com*, January 16, 2015, http://www.reuters.com/article/us-heart-failure-acceptance-idUSKBN0KP23X20150116).

6. Lana Barhum, "What Does It Mean to Accept Your Chronic Illness Diagnosis," 2, 3, https://theadventuresof arthritisnfibromyalgia.wordpress.com/2012/02/02/what-does-it-mean-to-accept-your-chronic-illness-diagnosis/. (Used with permission of the author.)

7. Thich Nhat Hanh, *The Heart of Buddha's Teaching: Transforming Suffering into Peace, Joy, and Liberation* (New York: Harmony Books, 2015).

8. Brad Zebrack (Introduction), and Mike Lang, "Valleys: Episode 4—Letting Go," *Huffingtonpost.com*, April 24, 2013, updated June 24, 2013, http://www.huffingtonpost.com/mike-lang/valleys-episode-4_b_3139143.html. (Used with permission of Brad Zebrack.)

9. Ted Wiard, "Valleys: Episode 4—Letting Go: Acceptance and Relocation," *Taos News*, June 27, 2013, 32.

CHAPTER 14

1. Amanda McBroom, "The Rose," lyrics copyright 1977 (Renewed) Warner-Tamerlane Publishing Company.

2. Rachel Rettner, "Why Older Adults Are Happier," *LiveScience.com,* May 29, 2013, https://www.livescience .com/34825-older-adults-happiness-negative-emotions.html.

3. Linda Lewis Griffin, "Accepting Change Gives Us Control as We Age," *Tribune,* March 10, 2015, http://www .sanluisobispo.com/living/family/linda-lewis-griffith /article39515499.html.

4. Mohtashemi, "Accepting Limits of Old Age."

5. Jaclyn Broadbent, Shikkiah de Quadros-Wander, and Jane A. McGillivray, "Acceptance Predicts Satisfaction in Later Life," *Springer,* July 2013, http:// www.springer.com/about+springer/media/springer+select ?SWID=0-11001-6-1427846-0.

6. Jennifer Reichstadt, Geetika Sengupta, Colin A. Depp, Lawrence A. Palinkas, and Dilip V. Jeste, "'Older Adults' Perspective on Successful Aging: Qualitative Interviews," *National Center for Biotechnology Information,* July 18, 2010, https://www.ncbi.nlm.nih.gov/pmc/articles /PMC3593659/.

7. "Can You Grow New Brain Cells?," Harvard Health Publications, October 2016, http://www.health.harvard.edu /mind-and-mood/can-you-grow-new-brain-cells; Lawrence Katz and Manning Rubin, *Keep Your Brain Alive: 83 Neurobic Exercises to Help Prevent Memory Loss and Increase Mental Fitness* (New York: Workman Publishing, 2014); Lisa Armstrong, "Neurobic tips: How to exercise your brain," October 8, 2013, *sheknows.com,* http://www .sheknows.com/health-and-wellness/articles/1016375 /neurobic-tips; Sandrine Thuret, "You Can Grow New Brain Cells. Here's How," *Ted Talk,* June 2015, https://www.ted .com/talks/sandrine_thuret_you_can_grow_new_brain_cells _here_s_how.

8. John Schappi, "Using The Serenity Prayer to Deal with Dementia," *Aging and Parkinson's and Me* (blog), May 5, 2011, http://parkinsonsand5htp.blogspot.com/search?q =serenity+prayer.

CHAPTER 15

1. This quote has frequently been attributed to both Confucius and Ralph Waldo Emerson. However, Irish novelist, essayist, and poet Oliver Goldsmith first used it in a book he wrote in 1760, *Letter from a Citizen of the World to His Friend in the East*. The book consists of a series of letters written by an imaginary Chinese traveler based in London named Lien Chi Altangi. The quote appears in letter VII in the book.

2. Becca Rose, "The Deep Importance of Learning to Accept Failure," *HelloGiggles.com,* February 21, 2015, http:// hellogiggles.com/learning-to-accept-failure/.

3. Michael Jordan, *People Weekly,* October 9, 1995.

4. Napoleon Hill, *Napoleon Hill's a Year of Growing Rich: 52 Steps to Achieving Life's Rewards* (New York: Plume, 1993), 109.

5. Allison Belger, *Had a Bad Day?—Now What? Psychologywod.com*, March 25, 2013, https:// psychologywod.com/2013/03/25/had-a-bad-day-now-what/. (Used with permission of the author.)

6. Susan Tardanico, "Five Ways to Make Peace with Failure," *Forbes.com,* https://www.forbes.com/sites /susantardanico/2012/09/27five-ways-to-make-peace-with -failure/#7438a3623640.

CHAPTER 17

1. From *Courage to Change,* page 183, copyright 1992, by Al-Anon Family Group Headquarters, Inc. Reprinted by permission of Al-Anon Family Group Headquarters, Inc. Excerpts from Al-Anon Conference Approved Literature are reprinted with permission of Al-Anon Family Group Headquarters, Inc. Permission to reprint these excerpts does not mean that Al-Anon Family Group Headquarters, Inc. has reviewed or approved the contents of this publication, or

that Al-Anon Family Group Headquarters, Inc. necessarily agrees with the views expressed herein. Al-Anon is a program of recovery for family and friends of alcoholics—use of these excerpts in any non-Al-Anon context does not imply endorsement or affiliation by Al-Anon.

2. *Ideonomy*, http://ideonomy.mit.edu/essays/traits.html.

INDEX

About the Author

Daniel A. Miller, JD, is the author of the best-selling *Losing Control, Finding Serenity,* a *Foreword Reviews* Book of the Year Award finalist. Like most compulsive controllers, Danny was always driven to succeed. He graduated from UCLA with honors in business administration and finished in the top 5 percent of his class at the UCLA School of Law.

While still in his twenties, he became a popular real estate instructor in the UCLA extension program, and in his thirties he wrote a critically acclaimed, best-selling professional book, *How to Invest in Real Estate Syndicates* (Dow Jones-Irwin, 1978). He later founded the California Institute of Real Estate Education, which offered state-licensed seminars to thousands of real estate professionals.

Financial success came early to Danny. Celebrities and other wealthy people entrusted him with large sums to invest on their behalf. By his midthirties he could afford to live in the exclusive Old Bel Air section of Los Angeles.

But for all his achievements and success, Danny had no sense of inner peace and serenity. He was imprisoned by his fears, anger, and anxieties—all bedfellows of controllers—and thus not open to the joy and wonders all around him.

After suffering a series of traumatic events and financial setbacks that he could not control—no matter how hard he tried—he finally began a new life journey based on letting go of control and accepting people and things as they are. He surrendered to the ups and downs and twists and turns of life instead of resisting them and trying to control people and events.

Over many years, he learned effective tools and strategies for letting go of control and accepting "what is" with his family and friends, as well as in sports, creative endeavors, and the workplace. In the process, he became an artist, a published poet, a champion senior tennis player, the author of a best-selling personal growth book, a happily married man, and a much wiser parent—all while cutting his work time by more than half.

Thus, through letting go of control and embracing life as it is, Danny found a different and more gratifying kind of success—an internal, core sense of well-being. He now writes and speaks about the profound benefits of letting go of control and practicing acceptance. His website features over seventy of his blog posts on control and acceptance dynamics, his poetry and paintings, and keynote speaker information.

Danny welcomes your comments and invites you to contact him:

Website: www.danielamiller.com
Facebook: https://goo.gl/2b1w8s
Twitter: https://goo.gl/3dptE5

A *Foreword Reviews* Book of the Year Award Finalist
and Six-Year Amazon Bestseller

From the Best-Selling Author of
The Gifts of Acceptance

LOSING CONTROL, FINDING SERENITY

How the Need to Control Hurts Us and How to Let It Go

Download a preview chapter at goo.gl/V8jmch

At work, they oversee every detail of every project and expect nothing less than perfection from their coworkers.

At home, they obsess over finding the "right" person. Then they criticize their lover or spouse for doing everything wrong.

As parents, they practice zero tolerance regarding their children's preferred study practices, choice of friends, clothing styles, and differing life views.

Sound familiar? Everyone knows the type: micromanagers, nitpickers, and domestic despots. Yet most people fail to recognize the signs of a compulsion to control in themselves—or realize the toll of their behavior on their career, their family, their friendships, and their own happiness.

In *Losing Control, Finding Serenity: How the Need to Control Hurts Us and How to Let It Go*, Daniel A. Miller pinpoints the dangers of excessive control. What's more, he shows those who feel the pressure to control how to break free and reap unexpected gifts. Sharing his journey of transformation, Miller reveals what happened when he finally decided to "surrender": his blinders fell away, new opportunities emerged, and he experienced unprecedented, profound inner peace.

Drawing on psychological insights, spiritual wisdom, and the real-life stories of acknowledged "control freaks," *Losing*

Control, Finding Serenity guides readers through an honest inventory of their control patterns—whether prodding, cajoling, withdrawing, playing the martyr, or intimidating—down to their roots. As most controllers will discover, their compulsion to control is provoked by deep-seated fears, anxieties, and insecurities and then aggravated by anger and resentment.

Filled with enlightening true stories, *Losing Control, Finding Serenity* gives readers the knowledge, courage, strategies, and "decontrol" tools to

- Identify and overcome the control triggers of fear, anger, and resentment
- Become a less domineering parent, build a family democracy, and reduce the struggles with children
- Find the right romantic partner and maintain a strong relationship by accepting who the person is rather than trying to change him or her
- Free one's creative flow and process
- Delegate to and trust coworkers to reap increases in productivity, efficiency, and job satisfaction—and reduce conflict and dissension
- Reduce codependency

In a chaotic, unpredictable world that's frequently beyond anyone's control, *Losing Control, Finding Serenity* offers welcome encouragement and validation for going with the flow of life as it is: an ongoing, ever-changing mystery.

Get Your Copy Today!

The ebook can be purchased at Amazon.com (goo.gl /B7mgTd), Apple iTune (goo.gl/9M8UN4), and Barnesandnoble .com (goo.gl/7iHmv1).

The print book can be purchased at Amazon.com (goo .gl/Gm7WBL), at Barnesandnoble.com (goo.gl/uVMFyk), and through your favorite bookseller.

7/18

CPSIA information can be obtained
at www.ICGtesting.com
Printed in the USA
FSHW01n1937060618
49138FS

9 780982 893050